"The Responsibility of the Church for Society"
and Other Essays by H. Richard Niebuhr

LIBRARY OF THEOLOGICAL ETHICS

Other Books in This Series

Basic Christian Ethics, by Paul Ramsey
Christianity and the Social Crisis, by Walter Rauschenbusch
Conscience and Its Problems, by Kenneth E. Kirk
Economic Justice: Selections from Distributive Justice *and* A Living Wage, by John A. Ryan
Ethics in a Christian Context, by Paul L. Lehmann
Feminist Theological Ethics: A Reader, edited by Lois K. Daly
The Holy Spirit and the Christian Life: The Theological Basis of Ethics, by Karl Barth
Love and Justice: Selections from the Shorter Writings of Reinhold Niebuhr, edited by D. B. Robertson
The Meaning of Revelation, by H. Richard Niebuhr
Moral Discernment in the Christian Life: Essays in Theological Ethics, by James M. Gustafson
Morality and Beyond, by Paul Tillich
Moral Man and Immoral Society, by Reinhold Niebuhr
The Nature and Destiny of Man: A Christian Interpretation (2 vols.), by Reinhold Niebuhr
Radical Monotheism and Western Culture: With Supplementary Essays, by H. Richard Niebuhr
Reconstructing Christian Ethics: Selected Writings, by F. D. Maurice
Religious Liberty: Catholic Struggles with Pluralism, by John Courtney Murray
The Responsible Self: An Essay in Christian Moral Philosophy, by H. Richard Niebuhr
Situation Ethics: The New Morality, by Joseph Fletcher
The Social Teachings of the Christian Churches (2 vols.), by Ernst Troeltsch
The Structure of Christian Ethics, by Joseph Sittler
The Ten Commandments, by William P. Brown
A Theology for the Social Gospel, by Walter Rauschenbusch
War in the Twentieth Century: Sources in Theological Ethics, edited by Richard B. Miller

"The Responsibility of the Church for Society" and Other Essays by H. Richard Niebuhr

Edited and with an Introduction by
Kristine A. Culp

Westminster John Knox Press
LOUISVILLE • LONDON

Book design by Sharon Adams
Cover design by Lisa Buckley

First edition
Published by Westminster John Knox Press
Louisville, Kentucky

This book is printed on acid-free paper that meets the American National Standards Institute Z39.48 standard. ♾

PRINTED IN THE UNITED STATES OF AMERICA

08 09 10 11 12 13 14 15 16 17 — 10 9 8 7 6 5 4 3 2 1

Library of Congress Cataloging-in-Publication Data

Niebuhr, H. Richard (Helmut Richard), 1894–1962.
  "The responsibility of the church for society" and other essays by H. Richard Niebuhr ; edited and with an introduction by Kristine A. Culp.— 1st ed.
      p. cm.—(Library of theological ethics)
  Includes index.
  ISBN-13: 978-0-664-23048-7 (alk. paper)   1. Church.   I. Culp, Kristine A. (Kristine Ann).   II. Title.
  BV600.3.N54 2008
  262—dc22

2007041812 P

Contents

Permissions

Library of Theological Ethics

General Editors' Introduction

The field of theological ethics possesses in its literature an abundant inheritance concerning religious convictions and the moral life, critical issues, methods, and moral problems. The Library of Theological Ethics is designed to present a selection of important texts that would otherwise be unavailable for scholarly purposes and classroom use. The series will engage the question of what it means to think theologically and ethically. It is offered in the conviction that sustained dialogue with our predecessors serves the interests of responsible contemporary reflection. Our more immediate aim in offering it, however, is to enable scholars and teachers to make more extensive use of classic texts as they train new generations of theologians, ethicists, and ministers.

The volumes included in the Library will comprise a variety of types. Some make available English-language texts and translations that have fallen out of print; others present new translations of texts previously unavailable in English. Still others offer anthologies or collections of significant statements about problems and themes of special importance.

We hope that each volume will encourage contemporary theological ethicists to remain in conversation with the rich and diverse heritage of their discipline.

ROBIN W. LOVIN
DOUGLAS F. OTTATI
WILLIAM SCHWEIKER

Introduction

The community of Christ is more actual, more present, less merely future, more powerful in our lives than we usually realize," H. Richard Niebuhr observed in 1953.[1] This was true of his own work as well: the theme of the actuality and power of Christian community was more pervasive in his writing than is usually realized. For Niebuhr, "faith" could not be adequately addressed without considering the community of faith; "history" took into account the internal narrative and moral reasoning of the community; "self" was a social self, accompanied by companions and situated in community.[2] His famous *Christ and Culture* typology is more exactly a typology of the relations of Christians and their communities with Christ and culture.[3] The community of faith appears as an orienting motif or perspective in all of his major published works. In addition, he wrote numerous essays on the reality of the church and its responsibility for society. This volume collects those writings for the first time. It presents what we can call H. Richard Niebuhr's theology of Christian community.

Niebuhr interpreted the church in relation and response to God and the world. Loyalty to Christ, gratitude to God, responsibility for the world,

---

1. H. Richard Niebuhr, "The Churches and the Body of Christ," 126, in this volume.

2. See H. Richard Niebuhr, *The Responsible Self: An Essay in Christian Moral Philosophy* (New York: Harper & Row, 1963; repr., Louisville, KY: Westminster John Knox Press, 1999); *The Meaning of Revelation* (New York: Macmillan, 1941; repr., Louisville, KY: Westminster John Knox Press, 2006); *Radical Monotheism and Western Culture: With Supplementary Essays* (New York: Harper & Row, 1960; repr., Louisville, KY: Westminster John Knox Press, 1993); and *Faith on Earth: An Inquiry into the Structure of Human Faith*, ed. Richard R. Niebuhr (New Haven and London: Yale University Press, 1989).

3. See H. Richard Niebuhr, *Christ and Culture* (New York: Harper & Row, 1951; repr., HarperSanFrancisco, 2001).

confession, conversion, reconciliation, love of God and neighbor—such themes patterned his thought. He addressed the reality of life before God, not the ideal nature of the church, and the responsibility of the church for society rather than its institutional form or its doctrines and beliefs. This approach was not only a matter of theological method; it was also an affirmation of God's continuing relation to the world as Creator and Spirit as well as Christ. Niebuhr rejected an ecclesiocentric interpretation of Christianity, attending instead to the triadic relation of church, world, and God. He rejected, too, an exclusively christocentric interpretation of the church in favor of a theocentric approach.[4]

Niebuhr pictured Christianity as a dynamic movement that exists before God in relation and response to the world. Christianity "must be understood as a movement rather than as an institution or series of institutions."[5] Moreover, the "church" cannot simply remove itself from the "world," as if it could thereby avoid contamination; nor does "church" simply descend into the "world," some sort of enfleshment of an unchanging ideal in historical institutions. "Church" and "world" are not strict opposites. When the church is defined only in opposition to the world, Niebuhr argued, then theologians cannot acknowledge aspects of common life that "relate positively to the world" as "agencies through which the grace of God as well as the power of sin may manifest itself." Indeed, when the church is defined only in opposition to the world, the likely result is an ideal church that is "invisible to our time" and, for all practical purposes, separated from the world.[6] Christianity as a movement involves both resistance to and affirmation of the world in an unending process of conversion of "church" and "world."

4. See H. Richard Niebuhr, "The Church and Its Purpose," (99–100); and "Reformation: Continuing Imperative," 143; both in this volume. Also see idem, "The Church Defines Itself in the World," 70, 73; and "The Doctrine of the Trinity and the Unity of the Church," 50–62; both in H. Richard Niebuhr, *Theology, History, and Culture*, ed. William Stacy Johnson (New Haven and London: Yale University Press, 1996).

5. H. Richard Niebuhr, "Christianity as a Movement," preface to *The Kingdom of God in America*, 50, in this volume. In coming to this interpretation, Niebuhr noted the influence of Henri Bergson's contrast between static and dynamic faith and of Karl Barth—perhaps Barth's contrast between faith and religion. The influence of longtime interlocutors Ernst Troeltsch and Josiah Royce seems probable as well.

6. See "The Church Defines Itself in the World," in *Theology, History, and Culture*, 70. This important essay (ca. 1958) is not included in the present volume because it is readily available. It surfaced the tacit and pragmatic choices involved in every theoretical work: "Definitions always represent decisions" (64). Niebuhr discussed the decisions that so-called "objective" or neo-orthodox theologies in fact make, including context-dependent ones and inconsistent ones. He downplayed his alternative proposals as "second thoughts," but they can be recognized as ideas central to his 1956 chapter "The Church and Its Purpose."

Four central aspects of Niebuhr's theology of Christian community will be explored in this introduction: the "method of polar analysis," the reality versus the ideality of the church, the purpose of the church as the increase of the love of God and neighbor, and the call for ongoing reformation. In addition, this exploration will serve to place Niebuhr's contributions in relation to his contemporaries and in an American strand of thought. The introduction concludes with comments on the organization of this volume.

THE METHOD OF POLAR ANALYSIS

Niebuhr did not define a fixed identity of the church, but located the movement of Christian faith dynamically between sets of polarities. At their best, Christian thought and churches express—move with, so to speak—the transforming reality of God in the world. This movement cannot be adequately represented in terms of synthesis (including Thomistic and Hegelian types), which assumes progress, or of dualism (either polarization or paradox), which implies stasis.[7] Rather, the ever-changing relation and response of church, world, and God can be more adequately presented with reference to abiding, yet ever shifting, sets of mutually interpreting and converting contrasts. He called this the "method of polar analysis."

In his 1956 book *The Purpose of the Church and Its Ministry*, Niebuhr identified a series of six polarities: subject (social-historical reality) and ultimate object (divine reality, the realm and rule of God), community and institution, unity and plurality, locality and universality, protestant and catholic, and church and world.[8] The six sets of poles represent different sorts of relationships: the first and final polarities are theological depictions of the church's relation to God and to the world, respectively. The remaining sets denote dynamic tensions that are internal to the church, some of which suggest the historic marks of the church. Thus there are intersecting relations between and among the poles, and the resulting multidimensional interaction is more

7. "Christianity as a Movement," 50–51. Niebuhr was already distinguishing synthesis, dualism, paradox, and transformative dialectic, later to be developed as ideal types in *Christ and Culture* (1951). Although Niebuhr had not yet articulated "the method of polar analysis" as such, the framework of nonresolving, nonidealistic, dialectic transformations was already there. He rejected a Hegelian construal of dialectic in favor of a Bergsonian approach. See Henri Bergson, *The Two Sources of Morality and Religion* (1935; Notre Dame, IN: University of Notre Dame Press, 1977).

8. "The Church and Its Purpose," 85–90. Notably, Niebuhr did not include a polarity of visible and invisible. For his deconstruction of that distinction, see "The Hidden Church and the Churches in Sight," in this volume.

like an ocean with changing tides and currents than like a channel flowing one direction. Each pole implies and requires its coordinate, but they are neither static nor polarized terms. Existing between and among the poles requires constant "rebalancing."[9]

For example, "protestant" and "catholic" represent abiding theological impulses of protest and affirmation in relation to the transcendence and immanence of God. They are "constituent element[s] in the being of the community, even apart from the institutional organizations." Each of the poles requires the other: "The Church cannot be protestant without being catholic." The protestant pole moves "away from the world that is not God," rejecting "all that is little because God is great." The catholic pole moves toward the world, affirming "the apparently insignificant because God is its creator, redeemer and inspirer."[10] Note that "protestant" is more than the negation of "catholic"—it includes affirmations of its own about the transcendence of God—and that "catholic" is not merely an institutional moment that is taken up in greater "protestant" synthesis, but affirms the incarnation of God in the world.[11] The church exists between both movements.

A similar polarity of iconoclasm and sanctification features prominently in Niebuhr's 1957 Montgomery Lectures, published as *Radical Monotheism and Western Culture*. This polarity summarizes enduring historical ethoi of Christian faith and holds being and value in relation. As the prophets and Puritans affirmed, God alone is holy: "No special places, times, persons, or communities are more representative of the One than any others are." Yet Christians have also affirmed "the sanctification of all things": all places, times, persons, and communities are created, and as such, good—indeed, "Whatever is, is good."[12] Only within this productive tension of being and value, of protestant principle and catholic vision, does monotheism become "radical." Radical

---

9. For the principle of balance, see part I of The Cole Lectures, "The Next Steps in Theology," in *Theology, History, and Culture*, esp. 8 and 18. "But when we think of the principle of balance, we do not think of the middle of the road but of that movement into the future which none of us can escape and which the church cannot escape. In the course of that movement, we are forever subject to the winds and tides. . . . The problem then is that of steering a steady course, not in defiance of the winds of doctrine, but in such a manner that we use their force to move to our goal" (18). For discussions of the polar method, see Jon Diefenthaler, *H. Richard Niebuhr: A Lifetime of Reflections on the Church and the World* (Macon, GA: Mercer University Press, 1986), chap. 4; and James W. Fowler, *To See the Kingdom: The Theological Vision of H. Richard Niebuhr* (Nashville: Abingdon, 1974; repr., Lanham, MD: University Press of America, 1985), esp. 27-29.

10. "The Church and Its Purpose," 89.

11. See H. Richard Niebuhr, "The Gift of the Catholic Vision," 113, in this volume.

12. *Radical Monotheism*, 52–53.

monotheism rejects all claimants to truth except God alone while also finding holiness in human beings and in all being. It relativizes all values in relation to the One source and center of value, while yet requiring that all beings be "met with reverence" because they have value. A radically monotheist faith is always changing, ever converting. "Faith in God involves us in a permanent revolution of the mind and heart, a continuous life which opens out into ever new possibilities. It does not afford grounds for boasting but only for simple thankfulness. It is a gift of God."[13]

Niebuhr's polar method and use of the polarity of protestant principle and catholic vision can be compared with Paul Tillich's well-known—and roughly similar—contrast of protestant principle and catholic substance, as well as with Tillich's polarities of God and the world. Indeed, it was Niebuhr's 1932 translation of Tillich's *The Religious Situation* that introduced Tillich's treatment of Protestantism as a critical principle to the United States.[14] Yet it would be a mistake to assume that Niebuhr merely appropriated Tillich's categories. The background to both of their work was Ernst Troeltsch's exploration of the relation of church-type and sect-type in the history of Christian thought, which in turn relied on Max Weber's ideal types. Tillich subsequently linked his use of polarities to Nicholas of Cusa's "coincidence of opposites"; his polarities can be understood to render Martin Luther's paradoxes in dialectical form. Niebuhr's engagement with Troeltsch is modified by the work of Henri Bergson; his polarities can be understood to recast the conversionist sensibilities of John Calvin and Jonathan Edwards.[15]

Niebuhr suggested a fully dialectical pattern of theological thinking in which contrasting positions neither simply oppose each other, nor are they readily resolved into each other, but continue to convert and generate among themselves. Such an ever-converting, generative approach yields a basic picture of the reality of life before God as an emergent field of tensions and transformations. This approach replaces a view of theology as offering a master strategy for resolving the ambiguity of the church and contrasts with efforts

13. Ibid., 126.

14. Paul Tillich, *The Religious Situation*, trans. and with an introduction by H. Richard Niebuhr (New York: Henry Holt, 1932). Niebuhr also reviewed the English translation of Tillich's *The Protestant Era*, trans. James Luther Adams (Chicago: University of Chicago Press, 1948), in *Religion in Life* 18 (1948): 291–92.

15. For recent assessments of Tillich's polarity of protestant principle and catholic substance, see Langdon Gilkey, *Gilkey on Tillich* (New York: Crossroad, 1990), 99; and Raymond F. Bulman and Frederick J. Parrekka, eds., *Paul Tillich: A New Catholic Assessment* (Collegeville, MN: The Liturgical Press, 1994): esp. Ronald Modras, "Catholic Substance and the Catholic Church Today"; Julia A. Lamm, "'Catholic Substance' Revisited: Reversals of Expectation in Tillich's Doctrine of God"; and Langdon Gilkey, "A Protestant Response."

focused on ensuring institutional or dogmatic stabilization. As we shall see, it also involved a shift from a focus on defining the ideal nature of the church to a broader concern with how Christian faith and community exist before God in companionship with and responsibility to the world.

AN AMERICAN STRAND OF THOUGHT

Niebuhr's work can be placed in an American strand of thought that insisted, against the prevailing European theologies of his day, that the social, historical character of Christian community is intrinsic to its being, indeed, is a means of divine interrelation with the world. Among contemporaries whose work can be located in this strand were Joseph Haroutunian, James Luther Adams, Howard Thurman, Claude Welch, Daniel Day Williams, and James M. Gustafson. Martin Luther King Jr.'s discussion of "beloved community" can be understood as closely related (see also the subsequent work of theologians such as James H. Evans Jr.). Arguably the work of Beverly Wildung Harrison and other feminist and womanist moral theologians such as Sallie McFague, Katie G. Cannon, and Margaret A. Farley represent an extension of this strand.[16]

In his classic study of American religious thought, historian William A. Clebsch observed that "the religious experience of Americans has been emphatically more voluntary than organic, more diverse than standard, more personal than institutional, more practical than visionary or (in that sense) mystical."[17] While Clebsch's generalizations did not emerge from these particular theologians, his characterization of the voluntary, varied, social-personal, practical character of religious reflection extends to their work. Their reflections typically begin with social-historical communities, structures, and patterns of relationship rather than with theological doctrines or biblical images. They situate the church within human life and understand both to be encompassed within an inclusive community that is built through the recon-

---

16. Several of these thinkers were and are in conversation with each other. Gustafson was first a student of Adams and then was Niebuhr's student, colleague, and with Williams, collaborator on the study of theological education that resulted in *The Purpose of the Church and Its Ministry*. Howard Thurman's *Jesus and the Disinherited* (Richmond, IN: Friends United Press, 1981) was said to have influenced King significantly. Harrison's dissertation was on Niebuhr, and his influences can be traced through her later work. Cannon's dissertation, written with Harrison, drew on Thurman and King together with resources from the life and work of Zora Neale Hurston. Farley studied with Gustafson.

17. William A. Clebsch, *American Religious Thought: A History* (Chicago and London: University of Chicago Press, 1973; Midway Reprint, 1984), 3.

ciliation of life to life and that recognizes an underlying unity and interdependence of life. Moral and theological thought thus has, in Niebuhr's construal, a triadic and reflexive character rather than a doctrinal structure. Christian community is interpreted (in all its ambiguity and promise) in the midst of its life with others in the world before God, rather than in extraction from the "world."

This acknowledgment that all life is before God can be contrasted with the idealist form of social mysticism represented by theologians who construed the church as a unity in faith. For example, Niebuhr's 1953 lecture, "The Churches and the Body of Christ," offered a decidedly different take on the metaphor of the church as body of Christ than did his contemporary, the Swiss Reformed theologian Emil Brunner. Brunner argued that theology should begin with the essential interrelation of faith and fellowship and then address the proper relation of fellowship in faith, what he called the *Ekklesia*, to the institutional church. He rejected an understanding of faith as mediated through institutional forms and practices; indeed, he suspected all outward and organized forms of ecclesial life.[18] Niebuhr, by contrast, explored the human quest for community that he saw expressed in the creation of religious movements in the present and through history. This he referred to as a quest for "the church beyond the churches." He cautioned against idealism, suggesting, as we have already noted, that "the community of Christ is more actual, more present, less merely future, more powerful in our lives than we usually realize." By the community of Christ he meant not primarily church institutions but rather "communities that exist in the minds, in the personalities and in the interpersonal relations" through common loyalties, memories, and hopes.[19] Niebuhr's invocation of the image of the body of Christ stresses the actual, mutual interdependence of Christians, not the mystical nature of their union in Christ.

Niebuhr's approach bore strong similarities to that of Joseph Haroutunian, the Chicago theologian and Calvin scholar, who critiqued the institutionalism and individualism of modern Protestantism.[20] Whereas Brunner interpreted

18. See Emil Brunner, *The Misunderstanding of the Church*, trans. Harold Knight (Philadelphia: Westminster Press, 1953); idem, *The Christian Doctrine of the Church, Faith, and the Consummation*, vol. 3 of *Dogmatics*, trans. David Cairns with T. H. L. Parker (1960; Philadelphia: Westminster Press, 1962).

19. "The Churches and the Body of Christ," 126–27. Here Niebuhr seems to develop the idea found in Josiah Royce of community as a time-process that exists through processes of interpretation that hold past memories and future hopes in common. In "The Church and Its Purpose," 87n3, Niebuhr explicitly challenged Brunner's anti-institutional interpretation of *Ekklesia*, arguing instead for the polarity of church as institution and as community.

20. See Joseph Haroutunian, *God With Us: A Theology of Transpersonal Life* (Philadelphia: Westminster Press, 1965).

the *Ekklesia* as an inward intersubjective immediacy that is always compromised by any social-historical form, Haroutunian emphasized the actual communion of believers and their witness in the world as a means of grace.
Likewise, James Gustafson's 1961 book, *Treasure in Earthen Vessels*, which first
took shape as his Yale PhD dissertation with Niebuhr, argued that the social,
historical, political, and meaning-making processes of human life are not "less
theological" than the church's confession of loyalty to Christ; indeed, such
processes are "means of God's ordering, sustaining, and redeeming his people."[21] The recognition of the theological significance of social patterns and
processes also set the stage for later feminist work. Social ethicist Beverly W.
Harrison later explained, "To speak of social relations is already to speak of
God-relations, and any conception of God-relations already implies patterns
of social relations."[22] Niebuhr and these others affirmed that the social, historical character of Christian community is not only intrinsic to its reality; it
is also a means of divine interrelation with the world. With this insight, they
also effectively retrieved John Calvin's construal of the church as an "external
means of grace"—albeit stressing its social-historical rather than its institutional reality—and his accent on ongoing transformation in history.

The call for reformation of the church and social transformation could not
be clearer in Niebuhr's work. His treatment of the church is first framed, in
The Social Sources of Denominationalism (1929), as a moral exposé of the accommodation of the churches to the "major social evils" of nationalism, racism,
and classism. His contributions to *The Church against the World* (1935) called
the church to depend on God alone for judgment and renewal in the face of
its "bondage" to capitalism, nationalism, and "anthropocentrism." In his 1937
historical study, he concluded that "the Kingdom of God in America" ought
not be understood as an unchanging ideal, but as a dynamic pattern that
emerges in the reality of Christian life and faith while yet remaining before
it.[23] This served to heighten, not lessen, the call for reformation.

Note that Niebuhr rejected the notion of one universal ideal in American
Christianity precisely at the point of affirming the social, historical reality of
churches as the means of their interrelation with God and the world. His 1945

21. James M. Gustafson, *Treasure in Earthen Vessels: The Church as a Human Community*
(Harper & Brothers, 1961; Chicago: University of Chicago Press, Midway Reprint, 1976),
13, 110.
22. Beverly Wildung Harrison, *Justice in the Making: Feminist Social Ethics*, ed. Elizabeth
M. Bounds et al. (Louisville: Westminster John Knox Press, 2004), 63.
23. As he later observed, whether one looked to the evangelical revival or the social gospel,
"theologically we have come to see that there never was a distinctively American point of
view from which the objects of theology could be peculiarly well seen or peculiarly well
interpreted" ("The Gift of the Catholic Vision," 109).

essay "The Hidden Church and the Churches in Sight" critiqued the pervasive modern emphasis on the ideality of the true church. By contrast, he suggested that the church "is an object of faith on which we rely as we do upon a friend, not as we depend—if we ever do depend—on an ideal in our mind or in a realm of essences." The church on which we rely, for example,

> is the holy company of those who receive a constant forgiveness and cleansing of their sins and who in measureless gratitude for measureless love forgive as they have been forgiven. It is the group of fellow workers in our time and in all times to come on which we rely to supplement and correct and remake our work so that it will be fit for eternity. . . . Such a Church is not an ideal. It is not the sort of thing we can strive to bring into existence, for it is before us.[24]

The church is "an emergent reality, hidden yet real." It emerges through the process of conversion, "which accompanies the whole of the Christian life." The conversion of the church, Niebuhr insisted (again with Calvin), is not substitution—or transubstantiation or deification—but reconciliation and restoration. "The gospel restores and converts and turns again; it does not destroy and rebuild by substituting one finite structure of life or thought for another."[25]

RECONCILIATION TO GOD AND NEIGHBOR

The purpose of church received memorable articulation as "the increase among men of the love of God and neighbor" in Niebuhr's 1956 study of theological education, undertaken in collaboration with Daniel Day Williams and James M. Gustafson. Niebuhr extended the beloved neighbor lavishly to encompass "all that participates in being." However, the neighbor is not simply humanity "in its totality," but rather "in its articulation, the community of individuals and individuals in community."[26] Similarly, his contemporary Howard Thurman, the pioneer in racial reconciliation, accented both the surrounding love of God and the particularity of love for fellow beings: "To speak of love for humanity is meaningless. . . . What we call humanity has a name, was born, lives on a street, gets hungry, needs all the particular things we need." According to Thurman, love for humanity

---

24. "The Hidden Church and the Churches in Sight," 57–58. See also the concluding paragraphs of *Faith on Earth*: "For the church in which we believe, on which we count as the supporting, interpreting community of faith, is actual, interpersonal reality, not a form, but an action, trust and loyalty experienced over and over again" (117).

25. "The Hidden Church and the Churches in Sight," 59–60.

26. "The Church and Its Purpose," 97.

involves an intrinsic interest in other persons and a "sense of their fact," that is, an awareness of each person's concrete accomplishments and plight combined with an imaginative sense of that person's potential.[27]

For Niebuhr, the central religious problem and the central moral problem are confronted in the concreteness and comprehensiveness entailed in this definition of the purpose of the church as the increase of the love of God and neighbor.

> The problem of man is how to love the One on whom he is completely, absolutely dependent; who is the Mystery behind the mystery of human existence in the fatefulness of its selfhood, of being this man among these men, in this time and all time, in the thus and so-ness of the strange actual world. It is the problem of reconciliation to the One from whom death proceeds as well as life, who makes demands too hard to bear, who sets us in the world where our beloved neighbors are the objects of seeming animosity, who appears as God of wrath as well as God of love. It is the problem that arises in its acutest form when life itself becomes a problem, when the goodness of existence is questionable, as it has been for most men at most times.[28]

Niebuhr explained elsewhere that "the movement beyond resignation to reconciliation is the movement inaugurated and maintained in Christians by Jesus Christ."[29]

Note that Niebuhr here was not far from the notion of "beloved community" developed by Josiah Royce and later adapted by Martin Luther King Jr. Royce insisted that community is the necessary matrix for complex individuality and a distinct "level of being," a well-ordered togetherness of distinct individuals that is more than a mere collective. Royce's 1913 book, *The Problem of Christianity*, offered the idea of "beloved community" as both a present social-spiritual reality, a "realm of grace" and the only bond that takes up the inevitable moral burden of the individual, and as the cause of universal community, to which individuals are bound through loyalty. Loyalty binds individuals together internally, not just functionally, in relation to a cause that may be realized only fragmentarily in history.[30] In the thought of Martin

---

27. Howard Thurman, *For the Inward Journey: The Writings of Howard Thurman*, selected by Anne Spencer Thurman (Richmond, IN: Friends United Press, 1984), 191–93, also 182. Thurman's writings and his cofounding of the interracial Church for the Fellowship of All Peoples in the 1940s called people to move across racial, ethnic, and religious barriers to find a "common ground" as beloved children of God.

28. "The Church and Its Purpose," 96.

29. "Responsibility and Christ," in *The Responsible Self*, 177.

30. Josiah Royce, *The Problem of Christianity* (1913; Chicago: University of Chicago Press, 1968), 206, 404. See also Royce's preface, 41.

Luther King Jr., "Beloved Community" expressed the interrelated structure of reality and envisioned a common destiny. "We are all caught in an inescapable network of mutuality, tied into a single destiny. Whatever affects one directly, affects all indirectly."[31] For King, love was the central moral imperative, and nonviolent resistance was love's practical counterpart and corresponding strategy; "Beloved Community" was both love's corporate expression and its end.

For Niebuhr, love of God and neighbor must be demonstrated directly through the church's social responsibility. This was especially clear in his 1946 essay "The Responsibility of the Church for Society," which attended to the despair and anxiety of the rapidly changing postwar period. The church in the United States "cannot announce the mercy of God without pointing out how this nation transgresses the limits assigned to men when it defrauds the Negro and refuses to condemn itself for the indiscriminate manner in which it made war in its use of obliteration bombing, or deals with defeated nations in the spirit of retribution rather than of redemption."[32] Moreover, the church must address the humble masses and not only governments and officials; it must address direct need as well as root causes. "This pastoral mission of the Church to the nations includes all those measures of large-scale relief and liberation which the times call for. It cannot be sufficient for the Church to call upon the governments of nations to feed the hungry and clothe the naked. Direct action is required here as elsewhere."[33] Finally, love of God and neighbor requires that the church "repents for the sin of the whole society and leads in the social act of repentance."[34] When the church follows Christ by accepting its social responsibility as a representative and pioneer for the whole world, "undivided by race, class, and national interests," then the reality of the church emerges through the demonstration of love of God and neighbor.

Here we might return to Clebsch's study of American religious thought. He traced the thought of "great exemplars," Jonathan Edwards, Ralph Waldo Emerson, and William James, arguing that "through different agencies each found the universe, for all its darkness and calamity, an eminently hospitable home for the human spirit." In answering this situation, "they

31. Martin Luther King Jr., "A Christmas Sermon on Peace" in *A Testament of Hope: The Essential Writings of Martin Luther King, Jr.*, ed. James Melvin Washington (San Francisco: Harper & Row, 1986), 254. Similar formulations appear in other writings.
32. H. Richard Niebuhr, "The Responsibility of the Church for Society," 72, in this volume.
33. Ibid., 73.
34. Ibid., 75.

came to derogate, on the one hand, systems of dogma and, on the other, to rise above psychoanalytic debunkings of religious behavior." Moreover, they "tried to divert American spirituality from its natural spillover into moralism by translating the religious impulse into being at home in the universe."[35] At the conclusion of his study, Clebsch turns to Niebuhr to summarize this legacy of thought,[36] and in Niebuhr's essays on the church we can see why Clebsch did. From the earliest essays in this collection to the last ones, Niebuhr returned to the problems of human division and alienation. "Man feels himself alone in an empty or inimical world over which chance or blind will presides," he observed in 1953. "He has no sense of being at home under the sky and upon the good earth; the earth is not his mother and there is no father in the heavens."[37] Accordingly, reconciliation to God correlates with reconciliation to life itself, engendering a sense of being at home in the universe: "Love to the Creator is love of being, rejoicing in existence, in its source, totality and particularity."[38]

CONTINUING REFORMATION

Yet if Clebsch correctly finds this legacy—of translating religious impulse into a sense of being at home in the universe—summarized in Niebuhr, for Niebuhr himself, translation wasn't enough. At the end of his career, he argued that resymbolization and reformation, not mere translation, were needed. To communicate the *reality* of life before God—of alienation and enmity, of malaise and despair, of the actuality of Christ, of the hope of healing and reconciliation, of a profound sense of being in love with life and the God of life—required resymbolization of religious sensibilities and reformation of the church.

"Our old phrases are worn out; they have become clichés by means of which we can neither grasp nor communicate the reality of our existence before God," he wrote in 1960.

---

35. Clebsch, *American Religious Thought*, 4, 3.
36. Ibid., 187.
37. "The Churches and the Body of Christ," 119.
38. "The Church and Its Purpose," 96. See also Niebuhr's 1962 Earl Lectures: "[Once] we were blind in our distrust of being, now we begin to see; we were aliens and alienated in a strange, empty world, now we begin sometimes to feel at home; we were in love with ourselves and all our little cities, now we are falling in love, we think, with being itself, with the city of God, the universal community of which God is the source and governor" ("Responsibility and Christ," in *The Responsible Self*, 177–78).

> Retranslation is not enough; more precisely, retranslation of traditional terms is not enough; "Word of God," "redemption," "incarnation," "justification," "grace," "eternal life"—is not possible unless one has direct relations in the immediacy of personal life to the actualities to which people in another time referred with the aid of such symbols.[39]

Niebuhr's 1961 Cole Lectures again addressed the need for resymbolization, proposing that "dialogue in the three-way conversation" of persons with God and with one another in the presence of God, rather than dogmatic proclamation, should be the real concern of faith. Apophatic or negative theology alone could not be the answer to the loss of vital symbols. He also called for a reengagement of religious affections, not that religion would become "amusement religion," but that the full range of knowing, relating, and communicating through emotions, arts, and values could be engaged.[40]

The call for the resymbolization of faith and reengagement of religious affections must be understood in relation to Niebuhr's call for the reformation of the church. As we have seen, this was not a new theme. "The relation of the church to civilization is necessarily a varying one since each of these entities . . . is subject to corruption and to conversion," he wrote in 1935. At that time he concluded, "The task of the present generation appears to lie in the liberation of the church from its bondage to a corrupt civilization."[41] In 1960 Niebuhr warned against "idolatries" *within* the church, especially tendencies to displace God with the church, to "deify" the Scriptures, and to substitute a "unitarianism of the second person of the Trinity" for God.[42] He instead called for "ecumenical vision": for reconciliation to God lived out through critical reconstruction of separate pasts (e.g., of Protestants and Roman Catholics) into a common, reconciled memory and through addressing the division and distrust of "the whole inhabited human world."[43] He sounded again the great theme of conversion or "permanent revolution" that resounds from Augustine, Calvin, and Edwards: "I still believe that reformation is a permanent movement, that *metanoia* is the continuous demand made on us in historical life."[44]

---

39. "Reformation: Continuing Imperative," 144.

40. The Cole Lectures, "The Next Steps in Theology," esp. 29–31, 34, 39. See also William Stacy Johnson's introduction to *Theology, History, and Culture*, xx–xxii.

41. H. Richard Niebuhr, "Toward the Independence of the Church," 22, in this volume.

42. "Reformation: Continuing Imperative," 143.

43. H. Richard Niebuhr, "Reconciliation in an Ecumenical Age," parts II and III, in this volume.

44. "Reformation: Continuing Imperative," 143.

"The Church is not responsible for the judgment or destruction of any beings in the world of God," Niebuhr wrote, "but for the conservation, reformation, redemption and transfiguration of whatever creatures its action touches."[45] Neither a triumphalistic nor a sectarian vision of Christianity suffices. A conversionist theology must foster dynamic, social-historical expressions of shared life that can be relied upon as means of God's grace. Furthermore, theology ought not to constrain divine creativity, reconciliation, and inspiration to special spheres of life. Rather, "the reformation of religion is the fundamental reformation of society."[46]

OVERVIEW OF THIS VOLUME

The essays selected for this volume represent some thirty years of Niebuhr's reflections on the reality of the church and its responsibility for society. The selections begin with the first chapter of his first book, *The Social Sources of Denominationalism*, published in 1929 while he was serving as professor and academic dean of Eden Theological Seminary in St. Louis, his denomination's theological school and his alma mater. Shortly after its publication, in 1931 and at age 37, Niebuhr returned to his PhD alma mater, Yale Divinity School, as an associate professor; later he was named the Sterling Professor of Theology and Christian Ethics. All of the other essays were written during his three decades at Yale. They were shaped not only by his teaching and immersion in the changing theological and social currents of the period, but also by his involvement in the changing face of American Protestantism as his own immigrant church, the German Evangelical Synod of North America, merged and then merged again eventually to create the United Church of Christ; by his participation in the emerging national and global ecumenical movement; and by the study of theological education that he directed in the mid-1950s in collaboration with Williams and Gustafson.[47] Some of the essays collected here were written for those particular contexts. The volume concludes with Niebuhr's own retrospective evaluation, written for the *Christian Century*'s "How My Mind Has Changed" series in 1960, just two years before his death on July 5, 1962.

The essays are grouped in three sections and in roughly chronological

45. "Responsibility of the Church," 67.
46. "Reformation: Continuing Imperative," 144.
47. For an interpretation of Niebuhr's triadic account of church, world, and God in relation to his study of theological schools, see W. Clark Gilpin, *A Preface to Theology* (Chicago: University of Chicago Press, 1996), chap. 4.

order. The first section, "Division and Disorder in the Church," contains the earliest selections. Note that Niebuhr's writing about the church was first framed in terms of the moral ineffectiveness of churches in the face of the "major social evils" of war, slavery, and social inequality. The problem, however, was not only "out there": social division and disorder run through the middle of the church and are inevitable insofar as Christianity always exists in civilization. The second section takes up "The Reality and Responsibility of the Church." Its subject matter includes Niebuhr's emphasis on Christianity as a movement and the emergence of his method of polar analysis, his affirmation of the church as a reality and not an ideality, and his powerful interpretation of the purpose of the church as the increase of the love of God and neighbor. The essays in the third section, "The Churches and the Whole Human Community," iterate the reality and responsibility of the church in relation to an "ecumenical vision" of the whole inhabited human world, and extend the themes of reconciliation and ongoing reformation to the wider world.

The reader who seeks a general sense of Niebuhr's theology of Christian community might start with "The Responsibility of the Church for Society" or "The Churches and the Body of Christ." Alternatively, the concluding essay, "Reformation: Continuing Imperative," offers Niebuhr's own assessment of his developing and abiding concerns. That said, the essays have greatest coherence when read in the roughly chronological order in which they have been arranged. While themes recur and build, there is surprisingly little repetition among the essays. That is not to say that the reader will find one overarching thesis and structured argument. This collection should be read "as the report of an inquiry more than as an argument for a set of propositions," as Niebuhr himself explained regarding Ernst Troeltsch's *The Social Teaching of the Christian Churches*. "To read in the way it was written is to accompany the author in his effort to understand a mass of historical data [here, the triadic relations of church, world, and God as lived and as borne in collective loyalties and memories] and to seek with him solutions of some intellectual and practical problems."[48]

KRISTINE A. CULP

---

48. H. Richard Niebuhr, "Introduction," to Ernst Troeltsch, *The Social Teaching of the Christian Churches*, 2 vols., trans. Olive Wyon (Chicago: University of Chicago Press, 1960), 7.

PART I

Division and Disorder in the Church

The time called particularly for the reformation of the church, and I was among those for whom this was the special task. As a convinced Protestant (not an anti-Catholic) who saw the sovereignty of God being usurped by the spirit of capitalism and nationalism, I felt strongly that the times called for the rejection of "Culture Protestantism" and for the return of the church to the confession of its own peculiar faith and ethos.

H. Richard Niebuhr, "Reformation: Continuing Imperative" (1960), reflecting on convictions that animated his work between 1930 and 1935

1

The Ethical Failure of the Divided Church [1929]

I

Christendom has often achieved apparent success by ignoring the precepts of its founder. The church, as an organization interested in self-preservation and in the gain of power, has sometimes found the counsel of the Cross quite as inexpedient as have national and economic groups. In dealing with such major social evils as war, slavery, and social inequality, it has discovered convenient ambiguities in the letter of the Gospels which enabled it to violate their spirit and to ally itself with the prestige and power those evils had gained in their corporate organization. In adapting itself to the conditions of a civilization which its founder had bidden it to permeate with the spirit of divine love, it found that it was easier to give to Caesar the things belonging to Caesar if the examination of what might belong to God were not too closely pressed.

This proneness toward compromise which characterizes the whole history of the church, is no more difficult to understand than is the similar and inevitable tendency by which each individual Christian adapts the demands of the gospel to the necessities of existence in the body and in civilized society. It has often been pointed out that no ideal can be incorporated without the loss of some of its ideal character. When liberty gains a constitution, liberty is compromised; when fraternity elects officers, fraternity yields some of the ideal qualities of brotherhood to the necessities of government. And the gospel of Christ is especially subject to this sacrifice of character in the interest of organic embodiment; for the very essence of Christianity lies in the tension which it presupposes or creates between the worlds of nature and of spirit, and in its resolution of that conflict by means of justifying faith. It demands the impossible in conduct and belief; it runs counter to the instinctive life of man and exalts the rationality of the irrational; in a world of relativity it calls for unyielding loyalty to unchangeable absolutes. Clothe its faith in terms of philosophy, whether

3

medieval or modern, and you lose the meaning of its high desires, of its living experience, reducing these to a set of opinions often irrelevant, sometimes contrary, to the original content. Organize its ethics—as organize them you must whenever two or three are gathered in the name of Christ—and the free spirit of forgiving love becomes a new law, requiring interpretation, commentary, and all the machinery of justice—just the sort of impersonal relationship which the gospel denies and combats. Place this society in the world, demanding that it be not of the world, and strenuous as may be its efforts to transcend or to sublimate the mundane life, it will yet be unable to escape all taint of conspiracy and connivance with the worldly interests it despises. Yet, on the other hand, Christian ethics will not permit a world-fleeing asceticism which seeks purity at the cost of service. At the end, if not at the beginning, of every effort to incorporate Christianity there is, therefore, a compromise, and the Christian cannot escape the necessity of seeking the last source of righteousness outside himself and the world in the divine aggression, in a justification that is by faith.

The fact that compromise is inevitable does not make it less an evil. The fault of every concession, of course, is that it is made too soon, before the ultimate resistance "to the blood" has been offered. Even where resistance seems to have gone to the uttermost the loyal man remembers that it might have been begun earlier, that it might have been continued a little longer, and that any compromise of the absolute good remains an evil. At last men must continue to condemn themselves not only for their failure to do what they could, but also for their failure to perform what they could not, for their denial of the absolute good whose categorical demands were laid upon their incapable will. But compromises are doubly evil when they are unacknowledged, when the emasculation of the Christian ideal remains undiscovered and when, in consequence, men take pride, as in an achievement, in a defeat of the essential gospel. Such unconscious hypocrisy not only bars the way to continued efforts to penetrate the stubborn stuff of life with the ethics of Jesus but is the author of further compromises made all too early. So it produces at last a spurious gospel unaware of its departure from the faith once delivered to the saints.

Denominationalism in the Christian church is such an unacknowledged hypocrisy. It is a compromise, made far too lightly, between Christianity and the world. Yet it often regards itself as a Christian achievement and glorifies its martyrs as bearers of the Cross. It represents the accommodation of Christianity to the caste-system of human society. It carries over into the organization of the Christian principle of brotherhood the prides and prejudices, the privilege and prestige, as well as the humiliations and abasements, the injustices and inequalities of that specious order of high and low wherein men find the satisfaction of their craving for vainglory. The division of the churches closely follows the division of men into the castes of national, racial, and economic groups. It draws the color line in the church of God; it fosters the misunderstandings, the self-exaltations, the hatreds of jingoistic nationalism by continuing in the body of Christ the spurious differences of provincial loyalties; it seats the rich and poor apart at the table of the Lord, where the fortunate may enjoy the bounty they have provided while the others feed upon the crusts their poverty affords.

II

The gospel's condemnation of divisiveness among men is one of its most characteristic and appealing elements. The spirit of Jesus revolted against Jewish class distinctions between the righteous few and the unhallowed many. He spoke to the outcast poor of the promise of the kingdom; he saw the typical child of God in a Samaritan who knew the meaning of human solidarity; ignoring the nationalism of Jews and Romans, he found faith superior to that of the chosen people in the heart of a centurion and sought his nation's glory in the rôle of a suffering servant. The ideal which was implicit in Jesus' teaching became explicit in Paul. Not only did this apostle refuse to recognize the religious differences between the parties of Peter, Apollos, Paul, and Christ, but—what is more important—he showed his converts that in Christ there can be neither Jew nor Greek, male nor female, bond nor free, and that with God there "is no respect of persons." Recognizing the diversity of gifts he resisted the ever-present tendency to find in diversity the excuse of division and he set forth that splendid theory of organic unity which remains for all time the ideal constitution of Christian society.[1] In James the spirit of equality in Christ again meets us in all his hearty condemnation of those who continue to observe in the service of the Lord those distinctions between rich and poor in which the world delights. The great Ephesian interpreter of the gospel recognized in Christ not only the divine Logos which informs the world with order but also the Son who is both child and brother, whose deep desire it is "that they may all be one," and the central meaning of whose teaching is interpretable only in the terms of sacrificing love.[2]

At this point, especially, the teaching of early Christianity met the wisdom of Stoic philosophers and the cosmopolitanism of the Roman world. The ideal became effective in the new church while it began slowly to penetrate into the social structure of the empire as a whole. The religious communism of the Jerusalem church, its surrender at the critical council of that stubborn sense of caste which barred the way to brotherhood between Jewish

1. 1 Corinthians 12.
2. John 17.

and Gentile Christians, the new attitude toward slaves expressed in the letter to Philemon and in the election of slaves to high office in Christian congregations, the sense of solidarity and equality which united masters and slaves and made Gentile disciples sacrifice their meager savings for the saints in Jewish Jerusalem, the communion meal itself with its lofty symbolism and its practical efficacy in overcoming the divisions of men—all these spoke of the reality of fellowship in Christ.[3]

Modern Christianity has returned with great enthusiasm to the study of this spirit and of these ideals of brotherhood. It has professed to find in them the solution of the difficulties and dangers of modern social life. The inequality of privilege in the economic order appears to the church to contain a fundamental denial of the Christian principle of brotherhood and to be symptomatic of an unhealthful state of society because it is contrary to the divine law inherent in the process of life as well as explicit in the gospel of Jesus. Nationalistic policies with their self-centered attitudes and their inevitable frictions, which culminate again and again in the bestiality of war—these also are subject to the church's strictures for all their cynical disregard of the Christian ethics and their appeal to the long-fostered sentiments of pride in one's own and contempt for another's national genius. The prejudice of racial caste-systems expressed on the one hand in the exclusion of Orientals from the privileges enjoyed by Occidental racial groups and in the social and political disabilities of the Negro, on the other hand in the fulsome praise of the superior qualities of Nordic tribes, seems no less contrary to the ideals of the Nazarene and to the spirit of the community he founded.

But a skeptic world notes with amusement where it is irreverent and with despair where it longs for a saving word, that the organization which is loudest in its praise of brotherhood and most critical of race and class discriminations in other spheres is the most disunited group of all, nurturing in its own structure that same spirit of division which it condemns in other relations. The world remembers that the idyllic unity of early Christianity was of but short duration: that Jewish and Gentile Christians, even in the days of Paul, often found their disagreements more significant than their agreements, their sense of race more potent than their sense of Christian solidarity. It recalls that Ebionites, Monarchians, Arians, Nestorians, and Monophysites were flung off, despised, and persecuted by the church in its great centripetal movement toward Catholicism. It notes that East and West and South and North, Slav and Latin and Teuton, have parted the garment of Christianity among them, unable to clothe a single body

3. Cf. [Adolf von] Harnack, *[The] Expansion of Christianity [in the First Three Centuries]*, vol. I, [trans. and ed. James Moffatt (New York: Putnam, 1904–05)], pp. 68–70, 181–249; [Ernst] Troeltsch, *Soziallehren der christlichen Kirchen und Gruppen* [1912], pp. 49–58.

of Christ with the seamless vesture of his spirit. It sees the Orthodox church of the East maintaining a specious unity by recognizing everywhere the national principle in the organization of Hellenic, Russian, Cyprian, Serbian, Rumanian, Bulgarian, and other virtually independent groups which do not even share a common name and which, in time of war at least, subject the principles of Jesus to the ethics of nationalism. The Catholicism of Latin Christianity, it appears, has made its politic adjustment to classes and nationalities and, more successfully than other representatives of the gospel, preserves unity in the bond of peace; but it does so by governmental more than by spiritual means; in times of crisis it shows itself pliant to the incessant demands of nationality and class; and it continues to suffer from the results of that great failure when its Roman-Italian heritage and interest showed themselves more powerful than its Christian ideal. If the attention is directed to the North and the West, to the successors of the Reformation, the surrender of Christianity to national, racial, and economic caste-systems becomes even more apparent. Here the ideal of brotherhood has not only yielded to the principle of nationalism but has suffered the latter to exploit it in the interests of parties and of rulers until at times the church has become a mere appendage of the state. Here Lutheranism is divided into German, Danish, Swedish, and Norwegian groups, while Calvinism observes the national boundaries in the organization of Swiss, French, German, Dutch, Scotch, and English churches. Here the races confess the same creeds, engage in the same forms of worship, nurture the same hopes, but do so in divided churches, where white and black find it easier to confess than to practice their common sonship to God. Here rich and poor meet in their separate cathedrals and conventicles that each may achieve salvation in his own way and that their class loyalties may not be violated by the practice of the ethics they profess.

Once Parthians and Medes and Elamites, Cretans and Arabians, the dwellers in Mesopotamia, in Judea and Cappadocia, Pontus and Asia, heard the common language of the gospel with a common joy. Now they and their modern heirs are without a common language; the joy of the great community has been lost in the bickerings, rivalries, and misunderstandings of divided sects. The accord of Pentecost has resolved itself into a Babel of confused sounds; while devout men and women continue devoutly to confess, Sunday by Sunday, "I believe in one, holy, catholic Church."

III

The orthodox explanation of this strange phenomenon in the church of brotherhood has been sought in the divergence of opinion between men as to the manner of their soul's salvation. That strange interpretation of the faith which has prevailed since the days when Greek disputants carried into it the problems and the methods of Greek philosophy, and which professes to believe that the salvation of men and nations is dependent on the maintenance of some opinion about metaphysical processes, has been responsible for many false analyses of the character and mission of Christianity. This typically Greek evaluation of the nature and function of ideas must be held in part accountable for the intolerance in religion which has given rise to many denominations through the exclusion of groups professing an opinion more or less divergent from that which had become established. But it is also responsible for obscuring the fundamental ethical problems of denominationalism by regarding all differences from a purely ideological point of view.

The orthodox interpretation of denominationalism in Christianity looks upon the official creeds of the churches as containing the explanation of the sources and of the character of the prevailing differences. Roman Catholics are defined, from this point of view, as Christians who hold to a semi-Pelagian view of sin and grace, believe in the innately effective character of the sacraments, recognize the primacy of the Roman bishop and hold to other cognate principles of faith and practice. Lutherans are distinguished, the interpreter of the creed tells us, by their belief in justification by faith alone, by their exaltation of the word of God as the primary means of grace, and by their profession of the priesthood of all believers. The Calvinist is marked by his views on predestination, on the legal character of the Bible, and on church discipline. Baptists are members of their denomination because they are convinced that believers' baptism by immersion is alone justifiable. Methodists are what they are because they temper an underlying Calvinism by Arminian modifications. As for the many subgroups to be found among Lutherans, Calvinists, Baptists, Methodists, these also vary from each other on one or another point of doctrine, which, it is said, explains their division and accounts for their antagonism. This mode of explanation has been popular since the time when Josephus described the Pharisees as a school of philosophers who maintained belief in the resurrection from the dead and in oral tradition, while the Sadducees were defined as those who held the opposite doctrines. The inadequacy of the explanation in this instance is patent. Certainly the Sadducees were not distinguished from the mass of Jewish people, or from the Pharisees, primarily by any religious opinions they held or failed to hold but by their social character as the members of the Hellenistic aristocracy; while back of Pharisaic ideas one looks for the fundamental element, for the racial loyalty which had its source in resistance to the Seleucid attempts to Hellenize Jewish civilization. Differences of opinion were surely present between Pharisees and Sadducees, but these differences had their roots in more profound social divergences. So it is with the Christian sects.

It is not possible to reduce all religious opinions and ideas to the category of rationalization, that is, to explain them as results of the universal human tendency to find respectable reasons for a practice desired from motives quite independent of the reasons urged. The psychology which regards all intellectual activity as such a rationalizing process is too patently one-sided to be able to maintain itself in the long run. Yet it is no less evident that much opinion or belief is in fact mere rationalization and that the reasons advanced for pursuing a given course of action are often far removed from the inspiring motive. This is true of many a political platform; it is true also of many a theological opinion. Again, many ideas which cannot be defined as rationalizations in the sense described are yet evidently secondary in character, representing the intellectual reflection of more fundamental social and cultural as well as religious conditions. An evident illustration of this relationship of ideas to underlying social conditions may be found in the attitude of Christians toward such institutions as private property, democracy, and slavery. Advancing and defending their positions on the basis of proof-texts drawn from the Scriptures, it has been possible for various sects to take antithetical views of the Christian or un-Christian character of these institutions. Only the purest novice in history will seek the explanation of such opinions in the proof-texts from which they purport to derive. In a similar fashion opinions as to church polity, varying from denomination to denomination, have been based in theory on New Testament reports of primitive church organization. The episcopal, the presbyterian, and the congregational forms have each been set forth as representing the original and ideal constitution of the Christian church. Yet the relationship of these forms to the political experience and desire of various groups is considerably more pertinent than is their relationship to the New Testament. Under the social and political conditions of the American frontier English presbyterianism, which had been convinced of its fidelity to the New Testament model, was almost unconsciously transformed into New England congregationalism, which now defended its form of organization as following the original and rightful Christian order. Episcopalianism was defended and attacked at many points in history, ostensibly because of its alleged maintenance of or departure from New Testament forms of church administration, but in reality because of its relationship to monarchical and absolute political government. The exaltation of the presbyter as the chief officer of the church, the endless quarrels as to the relative value of presbyterial and episcopal forms of polity, were supported by painstaking inquiries into the New Testament, by laborious definitions of Greek terms, by patient researches into the duties of non-Christian officials, who bore these titles before the church adopted the terminology. But the passionate conviction of the Calvinists that their form of organization was the right one had other sources than the savants' definitions of the meaning of "episcopos" or "presbyteros" in the Greek New Testament.

What is true of ethics and polity is true of theology. Less directly, but none the less effectively, theological opinions have their roots in the relationship of the religious life to the cultural and political conditions prevailing in any group of Christians. This does not mean that an economic or purely political interpretation of theology is justified, but it does mean that the religious life is so interwoven with social circumstances that the formulation of theology is necessarily conditioned by these. Where theology is regarded only from the ideological point of view, sight is lost of those very conditions which influence the divergence of its forms, and differences are explained on a speciously intellectual basis without taking into account the fundamental reasons for such variations. It is generally conceded that the theology of the first five centuries can be understood only if the psychology of the Greek mind and the social, religious, political, and economic conditions of the Roman Empire are apprehended in their relationship to the new faith. One will fail completely to understand Roman Catholicism if one blinds one's eyes to the influence of the Latin spirit and of the institutions of the Caesars upon its conception of Christianity and its formulation of doctrine. The spirit and the doctrines of Lutheranism derive not only from the New Testament but also from Luther's German temperament and from the political conditions of the church in Germany. Calvinism was no less influenced in its temper and theology by national character and by the interests of the economic class to which it especially appealed. Back of the divergences of doctrine one must look for the conditions which make now the one, now the other interpretation appear more reasonable or, at least, more desirable. Regarding theology from this point of view one will discover how the exigencies of church discipline, the demands of the national psychology, the effect of social tradition, the influence of cultural heritage, and the weight of economic interest play their rôle in the definition of religious truth. The importance of such elements is now generally recognized when the history of nations is under discussion. It is too often disregarded when denominational histories are written or sectarian differences investigated.[4]

IV

One element in the social sources of theological differentiation deserves especial attention. Max Weber and Ernst Troeltsch[5] have demonstrated how

4. Cf. [Werner] Sombart, *[The] Quintessence of Capitalism[: A Study of the History and Psychology of the Modern Business Man*, trans. and ed. Mortimer Epstein], [1911], pp. 267–268.

5. [Max] Weber, *Gesammelte Aufsätze zur Religionssociologie*, [vol.] I [Tübingen: J.C.B. Mohr (P. Siebeck), 1902], 153, 211; Troeltsch, *Soziallehren der christlichen Kirchen und Gruppen*, pp. 362ff.

important are the differences in the sociological structure of religious groups in the determination of their doctrine. The primary distinction to be made here is that between the church and the sect, of which the former is a natural social group akin to the family or the nation while the latter is a voluntary association. The difference has been well described as lying primarily in the fact that members are born into the church while they must join the sect. Churches are inclusive institutions, frequently are national in scope, and emphasize the universalism of the gospel; while sects are exclusive in character, appeal to the individualistic element in Christianity, and emphasize its ethical demands. Membership in a church is socially obligatory, the necessary consequence of birth into a family or nation, and no special requirements condition its privileges; the sect, on the other hand, is likely to demand some definite type of religious experience as a pre-requisite of membership.

These differences in structure have their corollaries in differences in ethics and doctrine. The institutional church naturally attaches a high importance to the means of grace which it administers, to the system of doctrine which it has formulated, and to the official administration of sacraments and teaching by an official clergy; for it is an educational institution which must seek to train its youthful members to conformity in thought and practice and so fit them for the exercise of rights they have inherited. The associational sect, on the other hand, attaches primary importance to the religious experience of its members prior to their fellowship with the group, to the priesthood of all believers, to the sacraments as symbols of fellowship and pledges of allegiance. It frequently rejects an official clergy, preferring to trust for guidance to lay inspiration rather than to theological or liturgical expertness. The church as an inclusive social group is closely allied with national, economic and cultural interests; by the very nature of its constitution it is committed to the accommodation of its ethics to the ethics of civilization; it must represent the morality of the respectable majority, not of the heroic minority. The sect, however, is always a minority group, whose separatist and semi-ascetic attitude toward "the world" is re-enforced by the loyalty which persecution nurtures. It holds with tenacity to its interpretation of Christian ethics and prefers isolation to compromise. At times it refuses participation in the government, at times rejects war, at times seeks to sever as much as possible the bonds which tie it to the common life of industry and culture. So the sociological structure, while resting in part on a conception of Christianity, reacts upon that conception and re-enforces or modifies it. On the other hand the adoption of one or the other type of constitution is itself largely due to the social condition of those who form the sect or compose the church. In Protestant history the sect has ever been the child of an outcast minority, taking its rise in the religious revolts of the poor, of those who were without effective representation in church or state and who formed their conventicles of dissent in the only way open to them, on the democratic, associational pattern. The sociological character of sectarianism, however, is almost always modified in the course of time by the natural processes of birth and death, and on this change in structure changes in doctrine and ethics inevitably follow. By its very nature the sectarian type of organization is valid only for one generation. The children born to the voluntary members of the first generation begin to make the sect a church long before they have arrived at the years of discretion. For with their coming the sect must take on the character of an educational and disciplinary institution, with the purpose of bringing the new generation into conformity with the ideals and customs which have become traditional. Rarely does a second generation hold the convictions it has inherited with a fervor equal to that of its fathers, who fashioned these convictions in the heat of conflict and at the risk of martyrdom. As generation succeeds generation, the isolation of the community from the world becomes more difficult. Furthermore, wealth frequently increases when the sect subjects itself to the discipline of asceticism in work and expenditure; with the increase of wealth, the possibilities for culture also become more numerous and involvement in the economic life of the nation as a whole can less easily be limited. Compromise begins and the ethics of the sect approach the churchly type of morals. As with the ethics, so with the doctrine, so also with the administration of religion. An official clergy, theologically educated and schooled in the refinements of ritual, takes the place of lay leadership; easily imparted creeds are substituted for the difficult enthusiasms of the pioneers; children are born into the group and infant baptism or dedication becomes once more a means of grace. So the sect becomes a church.

Religious history amply illustrates the process. An outstanding example is the "Half-Way Covenant" of the New England churches, which provided for the baptism of the children of second-generation, unconverted parents who had "owned the covenant" and submitted to the discipline of the church without being able to attain full membership because of their lack of the experience of salvation. The rise of "birth-right membership" in the Society of Friends shows the same process at work while the histories of Mennonites, Baptists, and Methodists offer further illustrations. Doctrines and practice change with the mutations of social structure, not vice versa; the ideological interpretation of such changes quite misses the point.

V

The evils of denominationalism do not lie, however, in this differentiation of churches and sects. On the contrary, the rise of new sects to champion the uncompromising ethics of Jesus and "to preach the gospel to the poor" has again and again been the effective means of recalling Christendom to its mission. This phase of denominational history must be regarded as helpful, despite the break in unity which it brings about. The evil of denominationalism lies in the conditions which make the rise of sects desirable and necessary: in the failure of the churches to transcend the social conditions which fashion them into caste-organizations, to sublimate their loyalties to standards and institutions only remotely relevant if not contrary to the Christian ideal, to resist the temptation of making their own self-preservation and extension the primary object of their endeavor.

The domination of class and self-preservative church ethics over the ethics of the gospel must be held responsible for much of the moral ineffectiveness of Christianity in the West. Not only or primarily because denominationalism divides and scatters the energies of Christendom, but more because it signalizes the defeat of the Christian ethics of brotherhood by the ethics of caste is it the source of Christendom's moral weakness. The ethical effectiveness of an individual depends on the integration of his character, on the synthesis of his values and desires into a system dominated by his highest good; the ethical effectiveness of a group is no less dependent on its control by a morale in which all subordinate purposes are organized around a leading ideal. And the churches are ineffective because they lack such a common morale.

The measure of their ethical weakness, of course, is taken especially in the crises, in wars and social revolutions. Divided against themselves they must leave the work of social construction to those forces which can develop an effective morale, which have for their basis the common and all too human interest in acquisition, in national and racial prestige, and which are unified by the common purposes and common fears of mankind at its lower levels. Under these circumstances it is almost inevitable that the churches should adopt the psychologically more effective morale of the national, racial, and economic groups with which they are allied. Hence they usually join in the "Hurrah" chorus of jingoism, to which they add the sanction of their own "Hallelujah"; and, through their adeptness at rationalization, they support the popular morale by persuading it of the nobility of its motives. The specifically Christian ethics is allowed to fade into the background while the ethics of the social classes takes its place, unless, indeed, it is possible to re-interpret the Christian ideal in such a way that its complete accord with social morality is demonstrated.

The lack of an effective, common, Christian ethics in the churches is illustrated by the manner in which they have divided their loyalties in each national crisis in the history of America and allied themselves with the struggling partisans of parliament and marketplace. During the American Revolution the rector of Trinity Church, New York, wrote to an English confrere, "I have the pleasure to assure you that all the society's missionaries without excepting one, in New Jersey, New York, Connecticut, and, so far as I learn, in the other New England colonies, have proved themselves faithful, loyal subjects in these try-ing times; and have to the utmost of their power opposed the spirit of disaf-fection and rebellion which has involved this continent in the greatest calamities. I must add that all the other clergy of our church in the above colonies though not in the society's service, have observed the same line of conduct." On the other hand, he testifies, the Presbyterian ministers, with sin-gular uniformity, are promoting by preaching and every other effort in their power "all the measures of the congress, however extravagant."[6] In any case, and this applies also to Congregationalists, Baptists, Methodists, and the other churches in the revolutionary colonies, one hears no word of a common Chris-tian system of values to which all can express allegiance. Each religious group gives expression to that code which forms the morale of the political or eco-nomic class it represents. They function as political and class institutions, not as Christian churches.

The case was not different in the slavery crisis. Methodism had carried an anti-slavery doctrine in its platform from the very beginning, but even White-field urged the desirability of eliminating from the charter of Georgia the pro-hibition of slavery and when Methodism became the church of the slaveholder as well as of the poor tradesman it soon divided into a Northern and a South-ern branch although the gradual emasculation of the anti-slavery clause in the old program was designed to maintain peace at the expense of principle. So it was also with Baptists and Presbyterians. Again the interests of economic class bent to their will the ethics of the Christian church and it was unable to speak a certain word on the issue of slavery. When the irrepressible conflict came the various denominations, as was to be expected, showed themselves to be the mouthpieces of the economic and sectional groups they represented.

The rôle played by the churches in the World War is too well known to require comment. Even when resistance was offered to war-time psychology it was often apparent that such resistance was not animated by Christian prin-ciples but by the social attitudes of immigrant groups, in whom the Old World heritage had not lost its force. Almost always and everywhere in mod-ern times the churches have represented the ethics of classes and nations rather than a common and Christian morality. Evident as this is in the crises, it is no less true of the times between crises. In the issues of municipal and national elections, on the questions of industrial relationships, of the conser-vation or abrogation of social customs and institutions—including the prohi-

6. *Ecclesiastical Records of the State of New York* [7 vols. (Albany, NY: J. B. Lyon, 1901–16)], vol. VI, pp. 4292f.

bition issue—the denominations have been the religious spokesmen of the special non-religious groups with which they are allied.

For the denominations, churches, sects, are sociological groups whose principle of differentiation is to be sought in their conformity to the order of social classes and castes. It would not be true to affirm that the denominations are not religious groups with religious purposes, but it is true that they represent the accommodation of religion to the caste system. They are emblems, therefore, of the victory of the world over the church, of the secularization of Christianity, of the church's sanction of that divisiveness which the church's gospel condemns.

Denominationalism thus represents the moral failure of Christianity. And unless the ethics of brotherhood can gain the victory over this divisiveness within the body of Christ it is useless to expect it to be victorious in the world. But before the church can hope to overcome its fatal division it must learn to recognize and to acknowledge the secular character of its denominationalism.

2

The Question of the Church [1935]

The title of our book [*The Church against the World*]¹ is not so much the enunciation of a theme as it is the declaration of a position. We are seeking not to expound a thesis but to represent a point of view and to raise a question. The point of view is from within the church, is that of churchmen who, having been born into the Christian community, having been nurtured in it and having been convinced of the truth of its gospel, know no life apart from it. It is, moreover, the point of view of those who find themselves within a *threatened* church. The world has always been against the church, but there have been times when the world has been partially converted, and when the church has lived with it in some measure of peace; there have been other times when the world was more or less openly hostile, seeking to convert the church. We live, it is evident, in a time of hostility when the church is imperiled not only by an external worldliness but by one that has established itself within the Christian camp. Our position is inside a church which has been on the retreat and which has made compromises with the enemy in thought, in organization, and in discipline. Finally, our position is in the midst of that increasing group in the church which has heard the command to halt, to remind itself of its mission, and to await further orders.

The question which we raise in this situation may best be stated in the gospel phrase, "What must we do to be saved?" The "we" in this question does not refer to our individual selves, as though we were isolated persons who could have a life apart from the church or apart from the nation and the race.

---

1. The book consisted of this introduction written by Niebuhr on behalf of his coauthors Wilhelm Pauck and Francis P. Miller, and three parts: "The Crisis of Religion," by Pauck; "American Protestantism and the Christian Faith," by Miller; and "Toward the Independence of the Church," by Niebuhr (also reprinted here). [Ed.]

It denotes rather the collective self, the Christian community. In an earlier, individualistic time evangelical Christians raised the question of their salvation one by one, and we cannot quarrel with them; they realized the nature of their problem as it appeared to them in their own day. Today, however, we are more aware of the threat against our collective selves than of that against our separate souls. We are asking: "What must we the nation, or we the class, or we the race do to be saved?" It is in this sense that we ask, "What must we the church do to be saved?" It is true that the authors of these brief essays have no commission to ask the question for others, nor to raise it as though they conceived themselves as spokesmen of the church. Yet they can and must ask it, as responsible members of the body of Christ, who believe that many of their fellow members are asking it also, and that the time has come for an active awareness of and discussion of its meaning.

The point of view represented and the question raised are to be distinguished, we believe, from those of many of our contemporaries who look at the church from the outside. Though some of these are members, yet they do not seem to be committed to the church, and they appear to direct their questions to it rather than to raise them as members of the community. They seem to criticize the church by reference to some standard which is not the church's but that of civilization or of the world. Apparently they require the church to engage in a program of salvation which is not of a piece with the church's gospel. They demand that it become a savior, while the church has always known that it is not a savior but the company of those who have found a savior. These critics have a right to be heard. A church which knows that it is not self-sufficient nor secure in righteousness but dependent on God for judgment and renewal as well as for life will expect him to use as instruments of his judgment the opponents and critics of Christianity. Yet the judgment of the outsider is not the final judgment of God, and his standard is not the divine standard for the church. An individual can profit greatly by the criticism of his fellows yet he will realize that they are judging him by standards which are neither his own nor God's, that he is both a worse and a better man than their judgments indicate, and that the greatest service they can render him is to call him back to his own best self. He will realize that he is not under any obligation to conform to the ideals which his friends or his critics set up for him, but that he is indeed obligated to be true to his own ideal. It is so with the church. Much as it may profit by the criticisms of those outside, it must not forget that they are asking it to conform to principles not its own, and endeavoring to use it for ends foreign to its nature. The question of the church, seen from the inside, is not how it can measure up to the expectations of society nor what it must do to become a savior of civilization, but rather how it can be true to itself: that is, to its Head. What must it do to be saved?

This question is not a selfish one; it is only the question of a responsible self. Critics of the gospel of salvation, who characterize it as self-centered and intent upon self-satisfaction, thoroughly misunderstand the sources and the bearing of the cry for salvation. In the period of individualism, persons sought redemption not because they desired pleasures in "the by-and-by" but because they found themselves on the road to futility, demoralization, and destructiveness. Because they were concerned with their own impotence in good works and with the harm they were doing to others, they were not less altruistic than those who were concerned only with doing good, and inattentive to the evil consequences of many good works. The avowed altruists were not less selfish than seekers after salvation just because they wished to be saviors rather than saved. Nor is it true that the desire for salvation is unsocial. It arises—for the church today as for individuals in all times—not in solitariness but within the social nexus. The church has seen all mankind involved in crisis and has sought to offer help—only to discover the utter insufficiency of its resources. Confronting the poverty, the warfare, the demoralization of human life, it has sought within itself for the wisdom and the power with which to give aid, and has discovered its impotence. Therefore it must cry, "What must I do to be saved?" It has made pronouncements against war, promoted schemes for peace, leagues of nations, pacts for the outlawry of war, associations for international friendship, organizations of war resisters; but the march of Mars is halted not for a moment by the petty impediments placed in its way. The church has set up programs of social justice, preached utopian ideals, adopted resolutions, urged charity, proclaimed good will among men; but neither the progressive impoverishment of the life of the many nor the growth of the privileges of the few has been stayed by its efforts. It has set up schemes of moral and religious education, seeking to inculcate brotherly love, to draw forth sympathetic good will, to teach self-discipline; but the progress of individual and social disintegration goes on. The church knows that the meaning of its life lies in the service it can give to God's creatures. It cannot abandon its efforts to help. Yet, looking upon the inadequacy and the frequent futility of its works, how can it help but cry, "What must I do to be saved?"

The question has another and more positive source. The church has been made to realize not only the ineffectiveness but the harmfulness of much of its labor. The individual raises the question of his salvation, rather than that of his saviorhood, when he faces the fact that he is not only not a Messiah but actually a sinner; that he is profiting by, consenting to, and sharing in man's inhumanity to man; that he is not the man upon the cross but one of the crowd beneath. So, the church has discovered that it belongs to the crucifiers rather than to the crucified; that all talk of becoming a martyr in the cause of good will, some time in the future, is but wishful thinking with little relevance to present reality. Its outside critics have taxed the church with giving opium to the people, and with securing its own position as well as that of its allies by preaching contentment to the poor. Had it been poor as Jesus was poor, had it identified itself with those to whom it preached contentment, had it not profited by the system of distribution which brings poverty, its conscience would have been clear. It would have been able to respond that it had preached nothing which it had not practiced. But being what it is, the church has been unable to refute the charge with a wholly good conscience. It knows that it has often been an obstruction in the path of social change and that it has tried to maintain systems of life which men and God had condemned to death. Its outside critics have held the church responsible for the increase of nationalism. They have pointed to the role of Protestantism, Pietism, and even of Catholicism in fostering the sense of national destiny, in giving religious sanction to the imperialist programs of kings and democracies, in justifying nationalist wars and in blessing armies bound on conquest. The church stands convicted of this sin without being at all confident that it has found out how to resist similar temptations in the future. At all events, it knows that it has been on the side of the slayers rather than of the slain. The critics have reminded the church of its part in the development of that economic system which, whatever its virtues, has revealed its vices so clearly to our times that none can take pride in having assisted it to success, in however innocent a role. The harm which the church has done and is doing in these and other areas of human life may be greatly exaggerated in its adversaries' indictments. But no section of the church can plead "not guilty" to all the counts. Convicted by its conscience more than by its foes, it joins the penitents at its own altars, asking, "What must we do to be saved?"

In the crisis of the world the church becomes aware of its own crisis: not that merely of a weak and responsible institution but of one which is threatened with destruction. It is true, as Francis Miller points out in his essay, that the church will probably survive in some form in any circumstances, and that the real question is whether it will survive as a reliable witness to the Christian faith. Yet it is also true that the larger question receives part of its urgency from the threat of extinction. It was when Israel's life as a nation was in danger that the prophets came to understand the more dire peril to Israel as a people of God. The knowledge of death played a part in the conversions of Augustine and Luther. So the church is being awakened to its inner crisis by the external one in which it is involved. It has seen enough of the indifference or hostility of the world, and of the defeats of some of its component parts, to realize that its continuance in the world is by no means a certainty. It knows the ways of God too well not to understand that he can and will raise up another people to carry out the mission entrusted to it if the Christian community fail him. It cannot look to the future with assurance that it carries a guarantee of immortality. The knowledge of the external crisis—in which as an institution it must become increasingly involved—may lead it to inquire first into the conditions of physical survival. Yet a society based, as the church has been, upon the conviction that to seek life is to lose it, must discover the fallacy in any attempt merely to live for the sake of living. Like any Christian individual faced with death, the church then realizes that the important question is not how to save its life but rather how to keep its soul, how to face loss, impoverishment, and even death without surrendering its self, its work, and its service.

From the point of view of civilization the question of the church seems often to be regarded as that of an institution which has failed to adjust itself to the world and which is making desperate efforts to overcome its maladjustments. The problem it presents is that of a conservative organization which has not kept abreast of the times, which has remained medieval while the world was growing modern, dogmatic while civilization was becoming scientific; which is individualistic in a collectivist period and theological in a time of humanism. The answer, it is thought, must come from science, politics, history, civilization. If the church is intent on being saved, then, from this point of view, it must direct its question to civilization. But within the church the problem has a different aspect. There is a sense, to be sure, in which the church must adjust itself to the world in which it lives and become all things to all men in order that it may win some. It is true also, within certain limits, that failure to adjust results in decay as is evident in all mere traditionalism. But the desire to become all things to all men still presupposes a faith which does not change and a gospel to which they are to be won. The failure of traditionalism, moreover, is less in its lack of adjustment to changing conditions than in the confusion of the spirit with the letter and in blindness to the actual shift of attention from meaning to symbol that has taken place within the church.

In the faith of the church, the problem is not one of adjustment to the changing, relative, and temporal elements in civilization but rather one of constant adjustment, amid these changing things, to the eternal. The crisis of the church from this point of view is not the crisis of the church in the world, but of the world in the church. What is endangered in the church is the secular element: its prestige as a social institution, its power as a political agency, its endowment as a foster-child of nation or of class. And this very peril indicates that the church has adjusted itself too much rather than too little to the world in which it lives. It has identified itself too intimately with capitalism, with the philosophy of individualism, and with the imperialism of the West. Looking to the future, the danger of the church lies more in a readiness to adjust itself to new classes, races, or national civilizations than in refusal to accept them. This moment of crisis, between a worldliness that is passing and a worldliness that is coming, is the moment of the church's opportunity to turn away from its temporal toward its eternal relations and so to become fit again for its work in time.

From the point of view of the church, moreover, the threat against it is being made not by a changing world but by an unchanging God. The "cracks in time" which now appear are fissures too deep for human contriving, and reveal a justice too profound to be the product of chance. The God who appears in this judgment of the world is neither the amiable parent of the soft faith we recently avowed nor the miracle worker of a superstitious supernaturalism; he is rather the eternal God, Creator, Judge, and Redeemer, whom prophets and apostles heard, and saw at work, casting down and raising up. He uses all things temporal as his instruments, but resigns his sovereignty to none. Hence the fear of the church is not inspired by men but by the living God, and it directs its question not to the changing world with its self-appointed messiahs but to its sovereign Lord.

Because this is true the church can raise the question of the church but cannot answer it. It knows where to go to hear the answer; it cannot specify at what time or in what way that answer will come: so that it will be compelled to obedience by the authority of the word and the conviction in its heart. It knows that it must go to the place of penitence. It knows that it must go into silence and quiet. It knows that it must go to the Scriptures, not in worship of the letter, but because this is the place where it is most likely to hear the reverberations of that commandment and that promise which sent it on its way. . . .[2]

---

2. A final paragraph has been omitted that commented on the relation of this essay to the other essays in the book. [Ed.]

3

Toward the Independence of the Church [1935]

The relation of the church to civilization is necessarily a varying one since each of these entities is continually changing and each is subject to corruption and to conversion. The history of the relationship is marked by periods of conflict, of alliance, and of identification. A converted church in a corrupt civilization withdraws to its upper rooms, into monasteries and conventicles; it issues forth from these in the aggressive evangelism of apostles, monks and friars, circuit riders and missionaries; it relaxes its rigorism as it discerns signs of repentance and faith; it enters into inevitable alliance with converted emperors and governors, philosophers and artists, merchants and entrepreneurs, and begins to live at peace in the culture they produce under the stimulus of their faith; when faith loses its force, as generation follows generation, discipline is relaxed, repentance grows formal, corruption enters with idolatry, and the church, tied to the culture which it sponsored, suffers corruption with it. Only a new withdrawal followed by a new aggression can then save the church and restore to it the salt with which to savor society. This general pattern has been repeated three times in the past: in the ancient world, in the medieval, and in the modern. It may be repeated many times in the future. Yet the interest of any generation of Christians lies less in the pattern as a whole than in its own particular relation to the prevailing civilization. The character of that relation is defined not only by the peculiar character of the contemporary church and the contemporary culture but even more by the demand which the abiding gospel makes upon Christianity. The task of the present generation appears to lie in the liberation of the church from its bondage to a corrupt civilization. It would not need to be said that such an emancipation can be undertaken only for the sake of a new aggression and a new participation in constructive work, were there not so many loyal churchmen who shy away at every mention of withdrawal as though it meant surrender and flight rather than renewal and reorganization prior to battle. Their strategy calls for immediate attack, as though the church were unfettered, sure of its strength and of its plan of campaign.

In speaking of the church's emancipation from the world we do not imply, as the romantic perversion of Christianity implies, that civilization as such is worldly, in the apostolic meaning of that term. Nor do we identify the world with nature as spiritualist asceticism does. The essence of worldliness is neither civilization nor nature, but idolatry and lust. Idolatry is the worship of images instead of that which they image; it is the worship of man, the image of God, or of man's works, images of the image of God. It appears wherever finite and relative things or powers are regarded as ends-in-themselves, where man is treated as existing for his own sake, where civilization is valued for civilization's sake, where art is practiced for art's sake, where life is lived for life's sake or nation adored for nation's sake. It issues in a false morality, which sets up ideals that do not correspond to the nature of human life and promulgates laws that are not the laws of reality but the decrees of finite, self-aggrandizing and vanishing power. Worldliness may be defined in New Testament terms as the lust of the flesh, the lust of the eyes, and the pride of life. As idolatry is the perversion of worship so lust is the perversion of love. It is desire desiring itself, or desire stopping short of its true object, seeking satisfaction in that which is merely the symbol of the satisfactory. It is pride, the perversion of faith, since it is faith in self instead of the faith of a self in that which gives meaning to selfhood. Such worldliness is far more dangerous to man in civilization than in primitive life because of the interdependence of developed society and the power of its units. The temptation to idolatry and lust is the greater the more man is surrounded by the works of his own hands. Moreover, every civilization is conditioned in all its forms by its faith, be it idolatrous or divine, so that it is difficult to draw a precise line between culture and religion. Nevertheless, Christianity regards worldliness rather than civilization as the foe of the gospel and of men; it rejects the ascetic and romantic efforts to solve life's problems by flight from civilization.

Idolatry and lust can be directed to many things. Worldliness is protean; understood and conquered in one form it assumes another and yet another. In contemporary civilization it appears as a humanism which regards man as existing for his own sake and which makes him the object of his own worship. It appears also as a nationalism in which man is taught to live and die for his own race or country as the ultimate worthful reality, and which requires the promotion of national power and glory at the expense of other nations as well as of the individuals with their own direct relation to the eternal. It has exhibited itself in the guise of a capitalism for which wealth is the great creative and redemptive power, and as an industrialism which worships the tawdry products of human hands as the sources of life's meaning. Humanity, nation, wealth, industry—these are all but finite entities, neither good nor bad in themselves;

in their rightful place they become ministers to the best; regarded and treated as self-sufficient and self-justifying they become destructive to self and others. In the modern world they have become ends-in-themselves. A culture which was made possible only by the liberation of men from ancient idolatries and lusts has succumbed to its own success. It is not merely a secular culture, as though it had simply eliminated religion from its government, business, art and education. It has not eliminated faith but substituted a worldly for a divine faith. It has a religion which, like most religion, is bad—an idolatrous faith which brings with it a train of moral consequences, destructive of the lives of its devotees and damning them to a hell of dissatisfaction, inner conflict, war and barbarism as lurid as any nether region which the imagination of the past conceived.

The church allied with the civilization in which this idolatry prevails has become entangled not only in its culture but also in its worldliness. This captivity of the church is the first fact with which we need to deal in our time.

I. THE CAPTIVE CHURCH

The church is in bondage to capitalism. Capitalism in its contemporary form is more than a system of ownership and distribution of economic goods. It is a faith and a way of life. It is faith in wealth as the source of all life's blessings and as the savior of man from his deepest misery. It is the doctrine that man's most important activity is the production of economic goods and that all other things are dependent upon this. On the basis of this initial idolatry it develops a morality in which economic worth becomes the standard by which to measure all other values and the economic virtues take precedence over courage, temperance, wisdom and justice, over charity, humility and fidelity. Hence nature, love, life, truth, beauty and justice are exploited or made the servants of the high economic good. Everything, including the lives of workers, is made a utility, is desecrated and ultimately destroyed. Capitalism develops a discipline of its own but in the long run makes for the overthrow of all discipline since the service of its god demands the encouragement of unlimited desire for that which promises—but must fail—to satisfy the lust of the flesh and the pride of life.

The capitalist faith is not a disembodied spirit. It expresses itself in laws and social habits and transforms the whole of civilization. It fashions society into an economic organization in which production for profit becomes the central enterprise, in which the economic relations of men are regarded as their fundamental relations, in which economic privileges are most highly prized, and in which the resultant classes of men are set to struggle with one another for the economic goods. Education and government are brought under the sway of the faith. The family itself is modified by it. The structure of cities and their very architecture is influenced by the religion. So intimate is the relation between the civilization and the faith, that it is difficult to participate in the former without consenting to the latter and becoming entangled in its destructive morality. It was possible for Paul's converts to eat meat which had been offered to idols without compromising with paganism. But the products which come from the altars of this modern idolatry—the dividends, the privileges, the status, the struggle— are of such a sort that it is difficult to partake of them without becoming involved in the whole system of misplaced faith and perverted morality.[1]

No antithesis could be greater than that which obtains between the gospel and capitalist faith. The church has known from the beginning that the love of money is the root of evil, that it is impossible to serve God and Mammon, that they that have riches shall hardly enter into life, that life does not consist in the abundance of things possessed, that the earth is the Lord's and that love, not self-interest, is the first law of life. Yet the church has become entangled with capitalist civilization to such an extent that it has compromised with capitalist faith and morality and become a servant of the world. So intimate have the bonds between capitalism and Protestantism become that the genealogists have suspected kinship. Some have ascribed the parentage of capitalism to Protestantism while others have seen in the latter the child of the former. But whatever may have been the relation between the modest system of private ownership which a Calvin or a Wesley allowed and the gospel they proclaimed, that which obtains between the high capitalism of the later period and the church must fall under the rule of the seventh and not of the fifth commandment, as a Hosea or a Jeremiah would have been quick to point out. The entanglement with capitalism appears in the great economic interests of the church, in its debt structure, in its dependence through endowments upon the continued dividends of capitalism, and especially in its dependence upon the continued gifts of the privileged classes in the economic society. This entanglement

---

1. The theory that modern capitalism is a system with a religious foundation and a cultural superstructure obviously runs counter to the widely accepted Marxian doctrine. It is not our intention to deny many elements in the Marxian analysis: the reality of the class struggle, the destructive self-contradiction in modern capitalism, the effect of capitalism upon government, law, the established religion. Neither are we intent upon defending the principle of private property as an adequate basis for the modern economic structure. But we are implying that modern capitalism does not represent the inevitable product of the private property system in which early democracy and Puritanism were interested, that it has corrupted and perverted that system, making of it something which it was never intended to be nor was bound to be. We believe that the economic interpretation of history is itself a product and a statement of the economic faith and that communism is in many ways a variant form of capitalist religion.

has become the greater the more the church has attempted to keep pace with the development of capitalistic civilization, not without compromising with capitalist ideas of success and efficiency. At the same time evidence of religious syncretism, of the combination of Christianity with capitalist religion, has appeared. The "building of the kingdom of God" has been confused in many a churchly pronouncement with the increase of church possessions or with the economic advancement of mankind. The church has often behaved as though the saving of civilization and particularly of capitalist civilization were its mission. It has failed to apply to the morality of that civilization the rigid standards which it did not fail to use where less powerful realities were concerned. The development may have been inevitable, nevertheless it was a fall.

The bondage of the church to nationalism has been more apparent than its bondage to capitalism, partly because nationalism is so evidently a religion, partly because it issues in the dramatic sacrifices of war—sacrifices more obvious if not more actual than those which capitalism demands and offers to its god. Nationalism is no more to be confused with the principle of nationality than capitalism is to be confused with the principle of private property. Just as we can accept, without complaint against the past, the fact that a private property system replaced feudalism, so we can accept, without blaming our ancestors for moral delinquency, the rise of national organization in place of universal empire. But as the private property system became the soil in which the lust for possessions and the worship of wealth grew up, so the possibility of national independence provided opportunity for the growth of religious nationalism, the worship of the nation, and the lust for national power and glory. And as religious capitalism perverted the private property system, so religious nationalism corrupted the nationalities. Nationalism regards the nation as the supreme value, the source of all life's meaning, as an end-in-itself and a law to itself. It seeks to persuade individuals and organizations to make national might and glory their main aim in life. It even achieves a certain deliverance of men by freeing them from their bondage to self. In our modern polytheism it enters into close relationship with capitalism, though not without friction and occasional conflict, and sometimes it appears to offer an alternative faith to those who have become disillusioned with wealth-worship. Since the adequacy of its god is continually called into question by the existence of other national deities, it requires the demonstration of the omnipotence of nation and breeds an unlimited lust for national power and expansion. But since the god is limited the result is conflict, war and destruction. Despite the fact that the nationalist faith becomes obviously dominant only in times of sudden or continued political crisis, it has had constant and growing influence in the West, affecting particularly government and education.

The antithesis between the faith of the church and the nationalist idolatry has always been self-evident. The prophetic revolution out of which Christianity eventually came was a revolution against nationalist religion. The messianic career of Jesus developed in defiance of the nationalisms of Judaism and of Rome. In one sense Christianity emerged out of man's disillusionment with the doctrine that the road to life and joy and justice lies through the exercise of political force and the growth of national power. The story of its rise is the history of long struggle with self-righteous political power. Yet in the modern world Christianity has fallen into dependence upon the political agencies which have become the instruments of nationalism and has compromised with the religion they promote. The division of Christendom into national units would have been a less serious matter had it not resulted so frequently in a division into nationalistic units. The close relation of church and state in some instances, the participation of the church in the political life in other cases, has been accompanied by a syncretism of nationalism and Christianity. The confusion of democracy with the Christian ideal of life in America, of racialism and the gospel in Germany, of Western nationalism and church missions in the Orient, testify to the compromise which has taken place. The churches have encouraged the nations to regard themselves as messianic powers and have supplied them with religious excuses for their imperialist expansions and aggressions. And in every time of crisis it has been possible for nationalism to convert the major part of the church, which substituted the pagan Baal for the great Jehovah, without being well aware of what it did, and promoted a holy crusade in negation of the cross. The captivity of the church to the world of nationalism does not assume so dramatic a form as a rule, yet the difficulty of Christianity in achieving an international organization testifies to the reality of its bondage.

Capitalism and nationalism are variant forms of a faith which is more widespread in modern civilization than either. It is difficult to label this religion. It may be called humanism, but there is a humanism that, far from glorifying man, reminds him of his limitations the while it loves him in his feebleness and aspiration. It has become fashionable to name it liberalism, but there is a liberalism which is interested in human freedom as something to be achieved rather than something to be assumed and praised. It may be called modernism, but surely one can live in the modern world, accepting its science and engaging in its work, without falling into idolatry of the modern. The rather too technical term "anthropocentrism" seems to be the best designation of the faith. It is marked on its negative side by the rejection not only of the symbols of the creation, the fall and the salvation of men, but also of the belief in human dependence and limitation, in human wickedness and frailty, in divine forgiveness through the suffering of the innocent. Positively it affirms the sufficiency of man. Human desire is the source of all values. The mind and the will of man are sufficient instruments of his salvation. Evil is nothing but lack of development. Revolutionary second-birth is unnecessary. Although some elements of the anthropocentric faith are always present in human society, and although it was represented at the beginning of the modern development, it is not the source but rather the product of modern civilization. Growing out of the success of science and technology in understanding and modifying some of the conditions of life, it has substituted veneration of science for scientific knowledge, and glorification of human activity for its exercise. Following upon the long education in which Protestant and Catholic evangelism had brought Western men to a deep sense of their duty, this anthropocentrism glorified the moral sense of man as his natural possession and taught him that he needed no other law than the one within. Yet, as in the case of capitalism and nationalism, the faith which grew out of modern culture has modified that culture. During the last generations the anthropocentric faith has entered deeply into the structure of society and has contributed not a little to the megapolitanism and megalomania of contemporary civilization.

The compromise of the church with anthropocentrism has come almost imperceptibly in the course of its collaboration in the work of culture. It was hastened by the tenacity of Christian traditionalism, which appeared to leave churchmen with no alternative than one between worship of the letter and worship of the men who wrote the letters. Nevertheless, the compromise is a perversion of the Christian position. The more obvious expressions of the compromise have been frequent but perhaps less dangerous than the prevailing one by means of which Christianity appeared to remain true to itself while accepting the anthropocentric position. That compromise was the substitution of religion for the God of faith. Man's aspiration after God, his prayer, his worship was exalted in this syncretism into a saving power, worthy of a place alongside science and art. Religion was endowed with all the attributes of Godhead, the while its basis was found in human nature itself. The adaptation of Christianity to the anthropocentric faith appeared in other ways: in the attenuation of the conviction of sin and of the necessity of rebirth, in the substitution of the human claim to immortality for the Christian hope and fear of an after-life, in the glorification of religious heroes, and in the efforts of religious men and societies to become saviors.

The captive church is the church which has become entangled with this system or these systems of worldliness. It is a church which seeks to prove its usefulness to civilization, in terms of civilization's own demands. It is a church which has lost the distinctive note and the earnestness of a Christian discipline of life and has become what every religious institution tends to become—the teacher of the prevailing code of morals and the pantheon of the social gods. It is a church, moreover, which has become entangled with the world in its desire for the increase of its power and prestige and which shares the worldly fear of insecurity.

How the church became entangled and a captive in this way may be understood. To blame the past for errors which have brought us to this pass is to indulge in the ancient fallacy of saying that the fathers have eaten sour grapes and the children's teeth are set on edge. The function of the present is neither praise nor blame of the past. It is rather the realization of the prevailing situation and preparation for the next task.

II. THE REVOLT IN THE CHURCH

The realization of the dependence of the church is widespread and has led to revolt. There is revolt against the church and revolt within the church. Both of these uprisings have various aspects. The revolt against the church is in part the rebellion of those who have found in Christianity only the pure traditionalism of doctrine and symbol which have become meaningless through constant repetition without rethinking and through the consequent substitution of symbol for reality. In part it is a revulsion against the sentimentality which substituted for the ancient symbols, with the realities to which they pointed, the dubious realities of man's inner religious and moral life. In part it is the revolt of those who see in the church the willing servitor of tyrannical social institutions and classes. On the one hand, the intellectuals abandon the church because of its traditionalism or romanticism; on the other hand, disinherited classes and races protest against it as the ally of capitalist, racial or nationalist imperialism. But these revolts against the church are not the most significant elements in the present situation, from the church's point of view. They represent desertions and attacks inspired not by loyalty to the church's own principles but rather by devotion to interests other than those of the church. Such desertions and attacks, however justified they may seem from certain points of view, serve only to weaken the church and to increase its dependence. Only a churchly revolt can lead to the church's independence.

The revolt within the church has a dual character. It is a revolt both against the "world" of contemporary civilization and against the secularized church. No other institution or society in the Western world seems to be so shot through with the spirit of rebellion against the secular system with its abuses, as is the church. No other institution seems to harbor within it so many rebels against its own present form. They are rebels who are fundamentally loyal—loyal, that is to say, to the essential institution while they protest against its corrupted form. They have no alternative religions or philosophies of life to which they might wish to flee. A few, to be sure, leave the church year by year, yet even among these[,] loyalty is often manifest. Some of the rebels remain romanticists who try to build "a kingdom of God" with secular means. More of them are frustrated revolutionaries who hate "the world" which outrages their consciences and denies their faith but who know of no way in which they can make their rebellion effective or by which they can reconcile themselves to the situation.

Like every revolt in its early stages, the Christian revolution of today is uncertain of its ends and vague in its strategy. It seems to be a sentiment and a protest rather than a theory and a plan of action. It is a matter of feeling, in part, just because the situation remains unanalyzed. It issues therefore in many ill-tempered accusations and in blind enthusiasms. Sometimes it concentrates itself against some particular feature of the secular civilization which seems particularly representative of its character. Perhaps the crusade against the liquor traffic was indebted for some of its force to the uneasy conscience of a church which was able to treat this particular phase of the "world" as the symbol and representative of all worldliness. As in all such emotional revolts there is a temptation to identify the evil with some evildoer and to make individual men—capitalists, munitions-manufacturers, dictators—responsible for the situation. Thus early Christians may have dealt with Nero, and Puritans with popes. The confusion of the revolt in the church is apparent, however, not only in its emotionalism but also in its association with revolting groups outside the church. In the beginning of every uprising against prevailing customs and institutions disparate groups who share a common antagonism are likely to assume that they share a common loyalty. It was so when princes and protestants and peasants arose against the Roman church and empire; it was so also when Puritans, Presbyterians, Independents and sectarians rose against King Charles. Dissenters and democrats united in opposing the established church in American colonies. Such groups are united in their negations, not in their affirmations. Their positive loyalties, for the sake of which they make a common rejection, may be wholly different. . . .[2] One danger to the Christian revolt is that it will enter into alliance with forces whose aims and strategies are so foreign to its own that when the common victory is won—if won it can be—the revolutionary church will be left with the sad reflection that it supplied the "Fourteen Points" which gave specious sanctity to an outrageous peace and that its fruits of victory are an external prosperity based on rotting foundations and debts which it cannot collect without destroying its own life.

The danger of such alliance or identification is not a fancied peril. The eagerness with which some of the leaders of the Christian revolt identify the gospel with the ideals and strategies of radical political parties, whether they be proletarian or nationalistic, the efforts to amalgamate gospel and political movements in a Christian socialism or in a Christian nationalism indicate the

2. Part of Niebuhr's elaboration of the "revolt in the church" is omitted here. [Ed.]

reality of the danger. It is not always understood by the American section of the Christian revolt that a considerable section of the so-called German Christian movement, in which the confusion of gospel and nationalism prevails, had sources in just such a reaction as its own against an individualistic, profit-loving and capitalistic civilization, and against the church in alliance with that civilization. There are many social idealists among these Germanizers of the gospel; and their fervor is essentially like that of the other idealists who equate the kingdom of God with a proletarian socialist instead of a national socialist society. The "social gospel," in so far as it is the identification of the gospel with a certain temporal order, is no recent American invention. In the history of Europe and America there have been many similar efforts which sought ideal ends, identified the church with political agencies, and succeeded in fastening upon society only some new form of power control against which the church needed again to protest and rebel. Christianity has been confused in the past, in situations more or less similar to the present, with the rule of the Roman Empire, with feudalism, with the divine right of kings, with the rule of majorities, with the dominance of the Northern States over the Southern, with the extension of Anglo-Saxon influence in the Orient. The confusion was as explicable and as specious in every instance as is the identification of Christianity with radical political movements today. Yet in every instance the result was a new tyranny, a new disaster and a new dependence of the church. It is one thing for Christians to take a responsible part in the political life of their nation; it is another thing to identify the gospel and its antagonism to the "world" with the "worldly" antagonism of some revolting group.

The common social ideal or hope of the West includes the establishment of liberty, equality, fraternity, justice and peace. Almost every revolting movement in the past as well as in the present has fought in the name of this ideal and sought to establish it. With the ideal, Christianity cannot but have profound sympathy, for Christianity taught it first of all to the Western world. But every political and social revolt is based on the belief that the ideal can be established through the exercise of power by a disinterested group or person, be it the feudal group, the monarch, the middle class or the proletariat. To identify Christianity with one form of the messianic delusion and of the philosophy of power, while rejecting another, is to be guilty of emotional and wishful thinking. In so far as every new revolt is an attack upon the philosophy and structure of power politics and self-righteousness, Christianity cannot but sympathize with it; in so far as it is itself a new form of the philosophy, Christianity must reject it or at least refuse to identify itself with it. So long, of course, as the church has no faith in a divine revolution and no strategy of its own for participation in that revolution it will need to commit itself to some other revolutionary faith and strategy or remain conservative. But in such a case it can have no true existence

as a church; it can function only as the religious institution of a revolting society, serving the interests of the society in the same way that a capitalist church
serves a capitalist society.

The revolt in the church faces another danger in consequence of the tendency toward the identification of Christianity with revolting secular movements. Multitudes of Christians who had become aware of tension between
the gospel and the world but who are also aware of the irreconcilability of the
Christian faith with the faiths of communism, socialism or fascism are forced
to make a choice between impossible alternatives. The greater part of them
are driven into reaction, for the old identification of Christianity with the prevailing "worldliness" is at least more familiar to them than the new. The fruit
of false action today in Christianity as in civilization will be reaction, not a true
revolution. Similar movements in the past offer unmistakable lessons on this
point. The confusion of Christian and of political Puritanism played no small
part in bringing on the Restoration. The identification of the protest against
slavery with the interests of the Northern States drove many Christians in the
South to the defense of the "peculiar institution," made the Civil War
inevitable and contributed to the continuation of the race problem. There is
no guarantee that reaction can be avoided under any circumstances, but it may
be held in check. There is no guarantee that overt struggle can be avoided, but
it is criminal to make civil, class or international war the more likely by confusing issues and by arousing the passions which religious fervor can awaken.
And in the end the solution will be as little to the mind of Christians as the
unsolved problem was.

The dangers and temptations which beset the Christian revolt offer no
excuse for acquiescence. The danger which confronts the world in the midst
of its idolatries and lusts is too real, the message of the church is too imperative, the misery of men is too actual to make quiescence possible. But the
moment requires the church to stand upon its own feet, to do its work in its
own way, to carry on its revolt against "the world," not in dependence upon
allies or associates, but independently. In any case the revolt in the church
against secularization of life and the system of "worldliness" points the way to
the declaration of its independence.

III. TOWARD THE INDEPENDENCE OF THE CHURCH

The declaration of the church's independence, when it comes, will not begin
on the negative note. A movement toward emancipation cannot become effective so long as it is only a rejection of false loyalties and entanglements. Loyalties can be recognized to be false only when a true loyalty has been discovered.

Moreover, independence is not desirable for its own sake. To seek it for its own sake means to seek it for the sake of self and to substitute loyalty to a self-sufficient self for loyalty to an alien power. But the church can have no illusion of self-sufficiency. Neither can it trust itself to play a messianic role in the deliverance of mankind. It knows too well that hierocracies have not been shining examples of justice among the aristocracies, monarchies, democracies, plutocracies, race tyrannies and class rules which have oppressed mankind.

The church's declaration of independence can begin only with the self-evident truth that it and all life are dependent upon God, that loyalty to him is the condition of life and that to him belong the kingdom and the power and the glory. Otherwise the emancipation of the church from the world is impossible; there is no motive for it nor any meaning in it. There is no flight out of the captivity of the church save into the captivity of God. Such words must seem to many to be pious and meaningless platitudes, mere gestures of respect to the past and bare of that realism which the present moment demands. That this is so is but another illustration of the extent to which the faith of the church has been confounded with the belief in the ideas, wishes and sentiments of men, and to which the word *God* has been made the symbol, not of the last reality with which man contends, but of his own aspirations. It remains true that loyalty to the "I am that I am" is the only reason for the church's existence and that the recovery of this loyalty is the beginning of true emancipation. It is even more true that this loyalty is not our own creation but that through the destruction of our idols and the relentless pursuit of our self-confidence God is driving us, in the church and in the world, to the last stand where we must recognize our dependence upon him or, in vainglorious rebellion, suffer demoralization and dissolution. The crisis of modern mankind is like the crisis of the prophets, the crisis of the Roman Empire in the days of Augustine, and that of the medieval world in the days of the Reformation. The last appeal beyond all finite principalities and powers must soon be made. It cannot be an appeal to the rights of men, of nations or religions but only an appeal to the right of God.

The appeal to the right of God means for the church an appeal to the right of Jesus Christ. It is an appeal not only to the grim reality of the slayer who judges and destroys the self-aggrandizing classes and nations and men. Such an appeal would be impossible and such a loyalty out of question were not men persuaded that this reality, whose ways are again evident in historic processes, is a redeeming and saving reality, and did they not come to some understanding of the manner in which he accomplishes salvation. But such persuasion and such revelation are available only through the event called Jesus Christ. If the church has no other plan of salvation to offer to men than one of deliverance by force, education, idealism or planned economy, it really has no existence as a church and needs to resolve itself into a political party or a school. But it knows of a plan of salvation which is not a plan it has devised. In its revolt it is becoming aware of the truth which it had forgotten or which it had hidden within symbols and myths. There is in the revolt something of the restlessness that comes from a buried memory which presses into consciousness. In some of its aspects it seems to be the blind effort to escape from the knowledge that the church along with the world belongs to the crucifiers rather than to the crucified. It seems to represent the desire to avert the eyes from the cross which stands in the present as in the past, and to turn attention away from ourselves to some other culprits whose sins the innocent must bear. When this memory of Jesus Christ, the crucified, comes fully alive it will not come as a traditional formula or symbol, reminding men only of the past, but as the recollection of a most decisive fact in the present situation of men. The church's remembrance of Jesus Christ will come in contemporary terms, so that it will be able to say: "That which was from the beginning, that which we have heard, that which we have seen with our eyes, that which we have beheld and which our hands have handled concerning the Word of life—that declare we unto you."[3]

Without this beginning in loyalty to God and to Jesus Christ no new beginning of the church's life is possible. But the self-evident truths and the original loyalties of the church can be recaptured and reaffirmed not only as the events in time drive men to their reaffirmation, but as the labor of thought makes intelligible and clear the vague and general perceptions we receive from life. The dependent church rejected theology or found it intelligible because it accepted a "theology" which was not its own, a theory of life which was essentially worldly. It wanted action rather than creeds because its creed was that the action of free, intelligent men was good and that God's action was limited to human agencies of good will. The revolters in the church are learning that without a Christian theory or theology the Christian movement must lose itself in emotions and sentiments or hasten to action which will be premature and futile because it is not based upon a clear analysis of the situation. They have learned from the communists that years spent in libraries and in study are not necessarily wasted years but that years of activity without knowledge are lost years indeed. They have learned from history that every true work of liberation and reformation was at the same time a work of theology. They understand that the dependence of man upon God and the orientation of man's work by reference to God's work require that theology must take the place of the psychology and sociology which were the proper sciences of a Christianity which was dependent on the spirit in man. The theory of the Christian revolution is beginning to unfold itself again as the theory of a divine determin-

---

3. 1 John 1–2. Niebuhr quotes from the Authorized Version. [Ed.]

ism, of the inevitable divine judgment, and of the salvation of men by the suffering of the innocent. But whatever be the content of the theory a clear understanding of it is needed for the work of emancipation, reorganization and aggression in the Christian community.

It is evident that far more than all this is necessary. There is no easy way in which the church can divorce itself from the world. It cannot flee into asceticism nor seek refuge again in the inner life of the spirit. The road to independence and to aggression is not one which leads straight forward upon one level. How to be in the world and yet not of the world has always been the problem of the church. It is a revolutionary community in a pre-revolutionary society. Its main task always remains that of understanding, proclaiming and preparing for the divine revolution in human life. Nevertheless, there remains the necessity of participation in the affairs of an unconverted and unreborn world. Hence the church's strategy always has a dual character and the dualism is in constant danger of being resolved into the monism of other-worldliness or of this-worldliness, into a more or less quiescent expectancy of a revolution beyond time or of a mere reform program carried on in terms of the existent order. How to maintain the dualism without sacrifice of the main revolutionary interest constitutes one of the important problems of a church moving toward its independence.

Yet it is as futile as it is impossible to project at this moment the solution of problems which will arise in the future. If the future is pregnant with difficulties it is no less full of promise. The movement toward the independence of the church may lead to the development of a new missionary or evangelical movement, to the rise of an effective international Christianity, to the union of the divided parts of the church of Christ, and to the realization in civilization of the unity and peace of the saved children of one God. The fulfillment of hopes and fears cannot be anticipated. The future will vary according to the way in which we deal with the present. And in this present the next step only begins to be visible. The time seems rife for the declaration of the church's independence. Yet even that step cannot be forced; how it will come and under what leadership none can now determine. We can be sure, however, that the repentance and faith working in the rank and file of the church are the preconditions of its independence and renewal.

4

The Disorder of Man
in the Church of God [1948]

I

At the outset of our effort to measure and understand the disorder of man in the Church of God we shall do well to remind ourselves of some general guiding principles.

First: we can rightly think and speak of this disorder only in the way of Christian repentance. There are many false and essentially disorderly ways of diagnosing what is wrong with the Church. Outsiders, for instance, may criticize it for failing to measure up to one of the various standards they employ. As nationalists or communists, as political liberals or political conservatives, as humanists, naturalists or idealists, they bring their particular notions of good and evil to bear on the Church and call on it to change its ways. Within the Church also there are ways of diagnosing and criticizing disorder which are not characterized by the spirit of repentance. Fault-finding directed towards other individuals or groups in the Church is one of these, for such fault-finding is as distinct from repentance as it is from brotherly admonition. Again, emotional shame, remorse and self-accusation in the Church do not always manifest "godly sorrow" working repentance, but may exhibit the "sorrow of the world" working death (2 Cor. 7:9–11). Repentance distinguishes itself from such an attitude in two ways. On the one hand it is an active turning away from sin rather than a morbid feeling. On the other hand it is hopeful, looking towards the healing of diseases, while remorse and shame, in so far as they remain worldly, are hopeless. Finally, there is a sort of self-criticism in the Church, which is not repentance in the Christian sense, because it is the counterpart of faith in the self rather than of faith in God. When we practise it we do so as those who believe that by means of one more effort to correct ourselves we shall overcome our disorder. In such repentance our chief disorder—our self-will, our determination to direct ourselves, our faith in ourselves—remains hidden from us. Christian repentance is the counterpart of Christian faith. As faith is the turning towards God in trust and reliance on Him, so repentance is the turning away from the self and its idols as the beings in which we have confidence and from which we expect our salvation. It is only in the spirit of such repentance and such faith that we can be bold enough in the Church to attempt to understand our sin.

Secondly: the disorder to which our attention is called in repentance is not so much the disorder *of* the Church as disorder *in* the Church. In certain ecumenical meetings held in the past representatives of some sections of the Church have objected to statements that the Church needs to repent, or that it is sinful. This objection has a true basis, recognizable by all of us who confess our belief in the Church as an integral part of our statement of faith in the Triune God. The Church as the community and Body of Christ, as the holy and whole people of God, as the City of God in heaven and on earth, is the mediator of grace and not of sin, of order and not of disorder. Disorder resides in ourselves and not in it. Yet disorder is in ourselves not as individuals only but also as organized parts of the Church, as vocational, national, ethnic and historical organs of its body. We are never merely individual church members but always also members of one of the special groups which constitute the whole community. It is in these groups as well as in our privacy that we hear the call to repentance. To-day we learn of our disorder not only as national or denominational parts of the Church, but also as the part of the Church located in the twentieth century.

Thirdly: we do well to remember that our disorder is not so much a state of affairs as an action of disordering, just as, on the other hand, order in the Church is not a static arrangement of its parts but the constant action of ordering by its Head. Individuals called to repentance by the Gospel sometimes seek to evade that call by reflecting that their sin is a state of miserable existence to which they have been reduced by earlier actions of their own or by the actions of their fathers. They ignore the fact that each repetition on their part of a disorderly action of the past involves a new consent of their wills, and that each repetition introduces fresh disorder into their lives. They also forget that they may be acting sinfully when they repeat in a present moment what was at one time right action but is no longer fitting, as when the mature man behaves in a way that was required of the child. In similar fashion organized members of the Church are tempted to place responsibility for present disorder on some action of their fathers. So sectarians tend to blame present church-disorganization on the Constantinian settlement, calling that the fall of Christianity, while Protestants may make the rise of the Papacy, and Roman Catholics the Reformation, the source of the Church's disorder. The call to repentance meets us in the Church not as those who are disordered by past actions, but as those who are disordering by present actions, whether these be repetitions of actions which were sinful in the past and are now sinful, or repetitions of actions which were done sincerely and in obedience to God by our fathers, but which we can only repeat in disobedience to Him.

Our fourth and final preliminary reflection is that man's disorder in the Church of God is a relative thing. As it is certain that we cannot in repentance know our sin without at the same time knowing in faith God's grace, so also it is certain that our disordering action in the Church is nothing absolute or independent, but is dependent on the presence of God's fundamental action of ordering. In the same vision in which we see the abundance of our sin we see the abundance of God's grace. If all were disorder there would be no Church at all. Where there is disease in the physical body, that is, disorder, there must also be health, that is, some right order; otherwise there would be no body at all which could live, even in diseased condition, and as fighting against its disease. This is the condition which we discern in the Church. Hence our repentance does not turn to despair, for it is the counterpart of that faith which knows the present action of divine grace. On the other hand our faith does not lead us into the temptation to become complacent and to accept our sin as inevitable or as not requiring repentance, for it is faith in the Saviour who rouses us out of our despair and our complacency with the question, "Wilt thou be made whole?" [John 5:6, AV].

II

When in such repentant faith and believing repentance we examine ourselves in the Church of God we become aware that there is no area of our existence in which sin does not seem to prevail. We are almost baffled by its pervasive, complex and radical nature. Yet we must seek to understand it. In this effort we may be assisted if we use the Scriptural analogy and regard the Church as the Body of Christ, made up of many members or organs. We note, then, that the disorder of man manifests itself in God's Church in at least four spheres: within the organs themselves, in the relations of the organs to each other, in the relations of the organs to the world, and, finally, in their relations to the Head. What in this complex confusion of disorder is symptom, what source or cause, we do not now inquire as we seek to know something of the extent of our distress.

We may regard the groups called denominations, national churches, vocational orders such as the clergy, local congregations and other associations of Christians, as organs of the body. What sorts of disorder are present in them? What sins abound in the intricate inter-relations of individual Christians to one another and to the organic unit? A factionalism like that described in

1 Corinthians doubtless appears in some, perhaps all, the organs. A loveless discipline which simply casts out offenders against the common rule marks the conduct of others. But perhaps the disorder of which we are most aware in many parts of the Church is the sin which is the opposite of both these former ones: loveless lack of discipline. We tend to purchase our unity at the price of principle and our peace with one another at the cost of genuine mutual service. This situation is connected with the character of the membership of our groups.

As in the days of Augustine "there are many reprobate mingled with the good and both are gathered together by the gospel as in a drag-net."[1] Yet we are forced to admit that the drag-net in our case has often been some other agency than the Gospel. Whether we have sought to expand our organizations in the Church through the direct political measures which created state churches, or have as free churches entered into competition for popular support with other Christian organizations and also with secular institutions, in any case, we have managed to bring into our churches many who have made no personal commitment to the Lord and His cause. When we contemplate what happened to the churches of Germany in their hour of sifting and winnowing, there are not many of us in other countries or in other Christian groups who can sincerely say that their membership contains a smaller proportion of the halfhearted, the luke-warm, of potential or actual deniers and traitors. It would doubtless be disorderly on our part to seek to anticipate the ordering action of the Lord of the Church Who sifts the wheat from the chaff on the threshing-floors of history, yet this does not excuse our more present disobedience both in continuing to gather into the Church those whom we do not call by the Gospel, and in withholding from those who have been so gathered adequate instruction and training in the exercise of genuine Christian vocation.

The first of these disordering actions brings into our churches many folk for whom "religion" is a part of a respectable life, or who pick and choose among the many "values" which the Church offers those which appeal to them. When, for the sake of meeting the wishes of such members, we withhold the challenge of the Gospel and turn it into an easy doctrine which demands no hard decisions, no continued self-denial in political and economic as in private matters, no surrender of the whole self to Christ, then we are guilty of the second part of this disorder. What in this realm is sincere adaptation to the needs of people, what self-deception, what is nominal and what is genuine Christianity, none of us can decide for others. Yet that there is much

---

1. Augustine, *The City of God* 18.49. [Ed.]

disorder here is patent, and that corporate as well as individual decisions about the conditions and requirements of church membership must be made seems also clear.

III

We have been made most acutely aware in our time of a second group of disorganizing actions in the Church, namely those which set the parts of the Church, the organic members of the Body of Christ, at variance with each other and so disturb, distract and inhibit the functioning of the whole body. These disorganizing actions of ours appear in various forms. Sometimes they are actions of self-isolation in which as local congregations, or as national and ethnic churches or as confessional groups we say in effect to other members of the Body of Christ, "We have no need of you." Again they are actions of conflict in which we contend against other parts of the body as though they were alien and inimical to the body itself. While this disorder seems particularly characteristic of the relations of the Protestant and Roman communities in the Church of Christ, it also appears in inter-Protestant and in Protestant-Orthodox relations. Again there are the disorganizing actions of those who seek special honour or prestige, as when a community of the clergy claim, or permit themselves to receive, a position in the Church which separates them from the lay orders. These various disorganizing actions may have a touch of imperialism in them, as when some one part of the Church undertakes to extend its rule over other parts, as though its own relations to the Head were more direct than that of the rest.

If the manifestations of disorder in these relations are manifold its roots seem to be manifold also. One apparent source is the social interplay in which action calls forth response in kind. As in the political sphere nationalism in one country calls forth nationalism in its neighbours, so, in the Church, self-sufficient denominationalism in one part tempts others to take the same attitude. Attack invites counter-attack so that anti-Romanism and anti-Protestantism, anti-liberalism and anti-orthodoxy flourish together. A second and more prevalent source of disorder lies in the confusion of a part with the whole. Thus a part of the Church regards itself as the whole or as representative of the whole, or it confuses the statement of what is most evidently true for it with the whole truth of the Gospel, or, again, it believes that the rule which it must follow in the performance of its function is the rule which the whole Church and all its other parts ought to follow. It may even believe that its particular function is the one function which the whole Church ought to carry out. Christendom is full of these confusions and so multiplicity of order is converted into disorder by the absolutizing of every relative, ordered pattern of action. The graciousness which marks some of the relations of distinct geographical, historical and vocational organs or groups in the Church is accompanied by much ingratitude to and for each other. We accept the correction, limitation and complementation of one by the other unwillingly and, rather than remain in the community of forgiveness and truly common faith, we separate from each other by withdrawal or excommunication.

These disorders among the organs of the Church appear most evidently in their external organization and even more in their lack of ecumenical order. They are, however, equally present and perhaps more destructive in the spiritual relations, as when in their prayers, their proclamation of the Gospel and their theological deliberation parts of the Church are either unmindful of one another or mind only those things in each other which invite correction. In this situation we impoverish ourselves as well as others, and as a result of our poverty have less and less to give to a world in need.

A multiplicity of special groups in the Church, serving men for God's sake in many diverse places and situations and cultures and performing many special functions, may be a sign of obedience to one Master and hence of order rather than of disorder. The presence in these congregations, denominations, and associations of many different special types of organization may also be indicative of such obedience. What is disorderly is isolation, contempt for each other, the pretension to special honour, the claim of the part to be the whole, the refusal to live in active inter-dependence, the effort to reign over others.

IV

The third sphere in which repentance discovers our human sin in the Church of God is in our relation as organized parts of the Church to the world outside the Church. Faith knows what action in this sphere is commanded by the Lord of the Church. Positively, our action is orderly when, following that command, we go into the world to make disciples of all nations, to baptize them and to teach them all that has been commanded to the Church. Negatively, it is ordered action when it is unspotted by the corruption and love of the world (Romans 12:2; James 1:27; 1 John 2:15). In the light of that double order we discern the confusion which has entered into our church-world relations. On the other hand, going into the world we become disciples of the world so that we import into the Church the corruptions of the world. Then in reaction to our secularism we are tempted to withdraw from the world and to seek holiness in isolation from it. Or, again, our ordered action in making disciples of Jesus Christ becomes the disordered action of those who seek to make converts to themselves rather than to Him and to teach such converts to observe not what our Lord has commanded us to do, but what we command them to do. Thus in our relations to the world we are tempted and often fall into the sins of secularism, of sectarianism, and of proselytism, using that last term to designate the sin which Jesus chastised when He said, "Woe to you, scribes and Pharisees, hypocrites! for you traverse sea and land to make a single proselyte, and when he becomes a proselyte, you make him twice as much a child of hell as yourselves" [Matt. 23:15, RSV].

The disorder of secularism is perhaps nowhere more apparent in our contemporary Church than in the extent to which we have permitted the order of the world to creep into the order of the Church. Having gone into the world of nations to make them disciples we have often accepted the order of nationalism, so that we not only remained silent before a nation's pretensions to the status of a chosen people, but have even fostered the illusion with our speech, for instance, about an "American theology" or perhaps even an American gospel in social form, or with our confusion of American and Christian "destiny."[2] In other instances we have so confounded Church and nation that we have regarded the former as an aspect of the latter. Again, the secular order and disorder of economic society have been accepted by the Church and been mirrored in its own order. So feudalism entered into the Church only to be displaced there by the capitalist order of a later time; and this in turn may make way for the socialist order. Whatever may be said for such orders of economic society as containing within themselves for their time and in their times elements of a natural order, the acceptance by the parts of the Church of secular gradations of rank, honour and wealth runs counter to its own order of mutual service. That it should carry out its mission to the men in the middle classes of capitalist society is doubtless a part of the Church's order, but that the mission should result in the formation of a middle-class church which defends the secular outlook and interests of that class is an evident corruption. That this disorder should lead to the demand for the formation of workers' churches which are to represent the secular as well as religious interests of another economic class is intelligible; yet the disorder in the latter case would be as deep as in the former. Perhaps the most painful disorder which has resulted and results from our conformation to the world is present where differences popularly and wrongly called "racial" have entered into the organization of the Church, so that worldly, anti-Christian, white and Gentile pride disfigures and

---

2. Note: Many specific examples of this disordering action can be given not only from the pages of theological writings, but also from home and foreign missionary appeals. But in an ecumenical Church each national group can best supply its own specific examples.

profanes the assemblies of Christians, by drawing caste lines even in worship services and at the Lord's Table, and by introducing "respect of persons" even into missionary and educational service.

The disorder in our church relations antithetical to this one is the sin of withdrawal from the world we are commanded to enter. It may be less manifest in external conduct in our day than it was in the days before the great series of monastic reforms and the Protestant Reformation. Yet it is present in other forms, as when we confess our faith only to each other's sympathetic ears in the Church and not before the world, or when we withdraw from the conflict with atheism in the world into our cells for the cultivation of our spiritual life, or when we disclaim responsibility for the political and economic disorders and sufferings of men because the Gospel relates us to another world than this one, or when we consent to the statement that "religion is a private matter."

As for the sin of "proselytism," though we may be inclined to regard the statement of Jesus about the making of proselytes as directed to men of another community than ours, we cannot wholly evade the indictment. We are aware that it has been difficult for us to distinguish between making disciples of Christ and making proselytes, between turning men to the Lord whose cause we seek to serve and turning them to ourselves who serve this cause. We have wanted men to become as we are, because we are Christians, and have confused the imitation of ourselves with the imitation of Christ. So in our relations to the Jews we have virtually demanded their acceptance of that Gentile Christianity which Paul freed from compulsory imitation of Jewish Christianity, while in our relations to the nations of the East we have found it difficult to dissociate our Western patterns of life and thought, of ritual and confession, from the pattern of Christ. Hence also we have carried into non-Christian countries divisions relevant to our culture but alien to theirs, and have with the Gospel exported also our spiritual disorders, and our secular, temporal order which for them has sometimes been a source of disorder.

V

In our repentance we are made aware that all our human wrongness in the Church is related to a disorder in our relation to its Head. On the one hand every unbrotherly act of which we are occasionally or habitually guilty in our relations to other parts of the Church and to the world outside is also, we must confess, an action of disobedience to Him. On the other hand it appears that every such disobedience is evidently rooted in something wrong in our relation to Him. We disobey Him because we do not trust Him. In faith we acknowledge Him as the risen Christ who gives us in our time His order and commandments; in doubt we think Him dead and believe that it is we who must give others His orders. So we arrogate to ourselves the right to rule His Church for Him. In faith we are assured that all power has been given to Him in heaven and on earth and that therefore we can, as we ought, make disciples of all nations; in our doubt of His power we adjust ourselves to all the ruling forces in the world, to the prejudices which hold sway over the minds of men, to their love of life and of status, to their worship of civilization and nation. In this adjustment we shift our faith from Christ to other saviours and other lords, though our tongues continue to confess His Lordship. In faith we accept the possibility and the reality of suffering with our Head and even learn to rejoice in it as a necessary element in our own and the world's salvation; in our doubt we shun suffering and perhaps fear even more to lead others into the fellowship of the cross. Hence our relations to the world are confused and confounded by the fear that we shall suffer if we proclaim and confess Christ before the hard-hearted, the mighty in knowledge or other strength, and by our anxiety that we may lead the humble and the weak into increased or additional sorts of suffering. So we become defensive or withdraw. In our faith we accept His orders to feed His lambs and His sheep in whatever particular situation He has called us; in our doubt we question His justice, fearing that others may receive a more exalted position than we, and, like Peter, we betray our jealousy of each other by asking, "Lord, and what shall this man do?" [John 21:21, AV].

Thus it is that in the same sphere in which our fundamental order as a Church appears, our fundamental disorder as members of the Church also becomes evident. Because we are ordered to the Head and by the Head of the Church therefore we are the Church and in the Church; because in this dis-ordered relation we doubt and disobey our Head, therefore, we are disordered in all our parts and in all our relations. Hence our sole but also our sure hope of salvation lies not in giving new orders to ourselves or to one another, but in the ordering which proceeds from Him Who rules us and calls us to ever new responses of free obedience. So we say, "Lord, we believe, help thou our unbe-lief," and in the measure of our faith do in our present what He commands, turning in sorrow from our disordering actions and in joy to His ordering.

PART II

The Reality and the Responsibility of the Church

The Church is not responsible for the judgment or destruction of any beings in the world of God, but for the conservation, reformation, redemption, and transfiguration of whatever creatures its action touches.

H. Richard Niebuhr, "The Responsibility of the Church for Society" (1946)

5

[Christianity as a Movement, 1937]

Preface to The Kingdom of God in America

In a previous study, *The Social Sources of Denominationalism*, I sought to discover the nature of the relation of religion to culture and to throw light on the complexity of American Christianity by examining the influence of social forces on faith and by tracing the sociological pattern of race, class and sectional interests as it manifested itself in the denominations. The account left me dissatisfied at a number of points. Though the sociological approach helped to explain why the religious stream flowed in these particular channels it did not account for the force of the stream itself; while it seemed relevant enough to the institutionalized churches it did not explain the Christian movement which produced these churches; while it accounted for the diversity in American religion it did not explain the unity which our faith possesses despite its variety; while it could deal with the religion which was dependent on culture it left unexplained the faith which is independent, which is aggressive rather than passive, and which molds culture instead of being molded by it. Furthermore, the only answer I was able to give to the problem of Christian disunity was in the form of a new appeal to good will to overcome stubborn social divisions and to incarnate the ideal of Jesus. This appeal seemed, upon critical reflection, to be wholly inadequate.

The pursuit of these and related problems led me to renewed study of American Christianity —although it is only as an amateur, as one who feels the need of testing the abstract ideas of theology and ethics in the laboratory of history, that I am able to pursue such studies. At first it seemed likely that the ideal of a kingdom of God on earth, which has played so great a role in recent religious thought and practice in this country, might offer a clue to the central intention, the common interest and the independent force of American faith. If Professor Kirk could deal with the ethics of Catholicism, despite its great variety, by tracing through early and medieval history the idea of the vision of God,[1] might it not be possible to use the idea of the kingdom on earth in similar fashion for understanding and interpreting American Christianity? Recent European writers, such as Adolf Keller and Heinrich Frick and many of those who participated in the discussions at Stockholm,[2] had seen in this idea the distinctive note in American Christianity and from their vantage point had been able to discern a unity in our religion which was hidden to the internal view. Furthermore, this idea seemed closely related to that "American dream" which James Truslow Adams had used so effectively in interpreting American history.[3] It appeared possible, then, that the expectation of the kingdom of God on earth was the great common element in our faith and that by reference to it one might be able to understand not only the unity beneath the diversity of American religion but also the effect of Christianity on culture. This expectation might be the hard, unyielding core which kept religion from becoming a mere function of culture; which enabled it to recover its initiative, to protest as well as to acquiesce, to construct new orders of life as well as to sanctify established orders; which accounted for its reformist activities, explained its relations to the democratic, antislavery and socialist movements, and its creativity in producing ever new religious groups.

This attempt to analyze American Christianity by means of this idea of the kingdom on earth failed. It was simply impossible to force Puritans, Quakers, and the great leaders and movements of the eighteenth and early nineteenth centuries into the mold of the modern social gospel. In them a *vis a tergo* rather than the attraction of an ideal seemed to be the moving force. They had a profound influence on culture but it was not the influence of direct attack. The result, however, was not wholly negative, for it appeared that although the earlier movements did not seek the kingdom on earth they were nevertheless intimately related to the social faith and that the latter was not as independent of traditional religion as it sometimes assumed. What the relationships were and

---

1. Kenneth E. Kirk, *The Vision of God: The Christian Doctrine of the Summum Bonum* (London and New York: Longmans, 1932). [Ed.]

2. Keller was an executive of church service agencies; Frick was a member of the theological faculty at Geissen, Germany. The Universal Conference on Faith and Life, held in Stockholm in 1925, brought together Anglican, Protestant, and Orthodox Christians who sought greater unity in Christian social witness in the aftermath of World War I. At the Stockholm conference, "Social gospel themes were pervasive and strongly pronounced; sustained talk of the kingdom of God was unprecedented." (Melanie A. May, "The Kingdom of God, the Church, and the World: The Social Gospel and the Making of Theology in the Twentieth-Century Ecumenical Movement," in Christopher H. Evans, *The Social Gospel Today* [Louisville, KY: Westminster John Knox Press, 2001], 38). [Ed.]

3. James Truslow Adams, *The Epic of America* (Boston: Little, Brown & Co., 1931). [Ed.]

what unity obtained in the whole process became clearer to me as I brought the insights of Bergson's great study of static and dynamic faith, of Barth and many another contemporary thinker to bear upon the subject.[4] In consequence I was led to certain discoveries in the field of American Christianity which were new to me.

The first of these was that the idea of the kingdom of God had indeed been the dominant idea in American Christianity just as the idea of the vision had been paramount in medieval faith—but it had not always meant the same thing. In the early period of American life, when foundations were laid on which we have all had to build, "kingdom of God" meant "sovereignty of God"; in the creative period of awakening and revival it meant "reign of Christ"; and only in the most recent period had it come to mean "kingdom on earth." Yet it became equally apparent that these were not simply three divergent ideas, but that they were intimately related to one another, and that the idea of the kingdom of God could not be expressed in terms of one of them alone. The social gospel with its emphasis on the kingdom on earth was building on the work of previous generations with their different emphases—emphases which had implied but not expressed the ideas or the faith of the subsequent movements. Kingdom on earth without sovereignty of God and reign of Christ was meaningless, as the last two were incomplete without it and without each other. If the danger of Puritanism lay in its effort to attain security by means of faith in divine sovereignty alone, and if the danger of Evangelicalism lay in the tendency to make sufficient the reign of Christ within all, the danger of the social gospel was in its idealism and in its tendency to deny the presuppositions on which it was based. Christianity, it appeared, could follow its grand line, avoiding the perils to right and left, if it remembered not only its goal but also its starting point and the middle of its course, the sovereignty of God and the revelation of his rule in Jesus Christ, crucified and risen from the dead.

Such is the theme of *The Kingdom of God in America*. It is a theme which cannot be developed in a single chapter and the scope of the argument appears only as the whole book is taken into account. This may seem to be an effort to present theology in the guise of history, yet the theology has grown out of the history as much as the history has grown out of the theology. As an interpretation it is selective in its choice of materials and in its emphases, yet it is an interpretation which has come out of the study of the materials, not an a priori design into which historical facts have been squeezed.

May I underscore some convictions which this study has fostered in me and

---

4. Henri Bergson, *The Two Sources of Morality and Religion* (New York: Henry Holt & Co., 1935). [Ed.]

which are even stronger than appears in the book? First is the conviction that Christianity, whether in America or anywhere else but particularly in Protestantism and in America, must be understood as a movement rather than as an institution or series of institutions. It is gospel rather than law, it is more dynamic than static. The genius of Christianity does not appear in its ethical programs any more than in its doctrinal creeds, important as they may be at times; these are abstractions from its life and become fetters when they are not recognized as abstractions. The true church is not an organization but the organic movement of those who have been "called out" and "sent." Institutionalized Christianity as it appears in denominations as well as in state churches, in liberal programs as well as in conservative creeds, is only a halting place between Christian movements. The Franciscan revolution not the Roman Catholic Church, the Reformation not the Protestant churches, the Evangelical revival not the denominations which conserved its fruits—and denied it—show what Christianity is. Since its goal is the infinite and eternal God, only movement or life directed toward the ever transcendent can express its meaning.

A second conviction is closely connected with the first. Christianity as a movement cannot be represented in terms of simple progress in either an otherworldly or a this-worldly direction nor can it be stated in terms of dualism, which always implies a static view. The relation of God to the world which is infinitely dependent upon him, but which nevertheless seeks to go upon an independent way, to a fallen world which remains the object of his redeeming love, requires of those who seek to be obedient to the divine imperative a dialectical movement. This dialectic is expressed in worship and in work, in the direction toward God and the direction toward the world which is loved in God, in the pilgrimage toward the eternal kingdom and in the desire to make his will real on earth. It is impossible to express the Christianity of the redemption in terms of a one-way movement toward the infinite and eternal God who draws men to himself, for this God so loved the world that he gave his only begotten Son for the world's salvation. It is equally impossible to express it in terms of love of the creature alone, for the meaning of the creature does not lie in itself but only in God. The life of the church as well as the life of Christian individuals illustrates this dialectical movement, and American Christianity illustrates it as much as any other. The evil habit of men in all times to criticize their predecessors for having seen only half of the truth hides from them their own partiality and incompleteness. Thought and faith remain fragmentary; only the object is one. A truly catholic Christianity does not seek a synthesis in which this dialectic can come to rest—only God can provide synthesis—but does its proper work in its own time with full recognition of the partial character of its interest and with full faith in the whole organic life which makes the partial work significant. The invisibility of the catholic church is due not only to the fact that no one society or nation of Christians can represent the universal but also to the fact that no one time, but only all times together, can set forth the full meaning of the movement toward the eternal and its created image. One of the great needs of present-day institutionalized and divided Christianity, perhaps particularly in America with its denominations, is recovery of faith in the invisible catholic church. The recognition of the dialectic character and of the continuity of the Christian movement is one aid to such a recovery. It helps us to tolerate, understand and love those who express another phase of the Christian movement than our own group expresses; it warns us of our own limitations, yet encourages us to do our own work with all our might and to seek unity not on the level of hazy sentimentalism but of the active intellectual and moral conflict of those who can contend faithfully because they share a common faith.

A final conviction is that American Christianity and American culture cannot be understood at all save on the basis of faith in a sovereign, living, loving God. Apart from God the whole thing is meaningless and might as well not have been. Apart from God and his forgiveness nationality and even Christianity particularized in a nation become destructive rather than creative. The history of the idea of the kingdom of God leads on to the history of the kingdom of God. Hence my greatest hope is that such a work as this may serve "even as a stepping stone" to the work of some American Augustine who will write a *City of God* that will trace the story of the eternal city in its relations to modern civilization instead of to ancient Rome, or of Jonathan Edwards *redivivus* who will bring down to our own time the *History of the Work of Redemption*.

6

The Hidden Church and
the Churches in Sight [1945]

Men who love the Church always find it confusing and painful to contemplate the contradictions between the reality they love and the religious organizations which are called by the same name. It is painful because these organizations seem antithetical and even inimical to what the Church means. It is confusing because the Church is so closely bound up with them that one cannot serve it without working in and through and for them. The confusion is the more distressing and the pain the more acute in a time when the failures of human institutions and the greatness of man's need direct attention more than ever to the Church, increasing our longing for its appearance and our desire to establish it. In this situation both the reinforcement of our confidence and the reformation of action wait upon the clarification of thought, and it is necessary that from many points of view, with the aid of many instruments of analysis, that the relationship of the Church to the churches be re-examined and reinterpreted.

If there is to be genuine clarification it is desirable, surely, that we do not slur over and minimize, as we so easily do, the real contradictions which obtain between the Church of faith and the so-called churches, that is, all those local, national, and international organizations which form part of our weekly if not daily experience. The Church of faith is the one to which Christians refer when we repeat our creed and say, "I believe in the Holy Catholic Church" or "in the one holy Catholic and Apostolic Church." It is the Church which we have in mind when we hear the Scriptures read, attending to Jesus' words about the rock on which he will build his Church or to Paul's parable about the body and its members. We sing about it in our hymns, saying that "The Church's one foundation is Jesus Christ, her Lord," rejoicing in the glorious things which are spoken of her and affirming our love of "the Church our blest Redeemer saved with his own precious blood." It is one and holy and universal and Christian.

But the churches which we organize, support, and defend against adversaries, whose doings are reported in the daily newspapers and weekly magazines, which form as intimate a part of our civilization as stores and schools and barber shops—these are another matter. It is quite unnecessary to remind ourselves again of their disunity and their lack of universality. They are not only divided but divisive, splitting our human societies into incompatible segments. Every village, city, nation, and the whole planet itself bear witness to the fact that the churches are not one and are not making mankind one. Their lack of holiness has been remarked upon age after age, within and without; it has led to reformation after reformation and schism after schism with the consequence that newly constituted groups became guilty either of a new secularism or a new self-righteousness—that caricature of holiness to which profaneness is often preferable.

The name Christian can indeed be applied to the churches but only in a very special sense; it is a family name rather than a descriptive adjective. The churches claim descent from Christ and seem entitled to that claim in a manner analogous to the one in which some "Mayflower" descendant is entitled to claim a Pilgrim as his ancestor. In his case it may be estimated that he had some 512 ancestors living in 1620; choosing that one of this number who is most honorable, he claims him as his progenitor to the neglect of 511 other forbears. So our churches, the religious organizations of the Western world, have multitudinous ancestors but they hang only the picture of Jesus Christ on the walls of their homes. Their physical and mental equipment, however, shows how various is their heritage. Our religious rites, our intellectual systems, our forms of organization, our codes of conduct and all the other features of our common life have come to us from many sources and we find it impossible to show how these features are in reality all derived from Jesus Christ—either after the flesh or after the spirit. As a religion our Christianity is a highly syncretistic thing which has borrowed or received elements from many quarters. And what is true of Christianity in general is true of all its particular forms. It is not hard to trace the ancestry of the Roman Catholic Church to other fathers besides the apostles nor to discover that the Protestant churches are the product of other forces besides the gospel; the sects which have flourished in all times usually claim a virgin birth but it is not difficult to discern that they were conceived with the help of a mundane paternity co-operating with the spirit of Christ. Roman Empire and Roman law, Greek philosophy and Gnostic speculation, mystery religions and household faiths, feudal policy and Germanic ideas of law, rising individualism and new industrialism, nationalism and capitalism, technology and science—all these and many more have so conditioned the churches that not one of them can credibly maintain that the only or even the chief influence in its life is that of Jesus Christ. If moral characteristics such as humility, obedience to God, and self-sacrifice are taken into account, the problem of the relation of the churches to Christ does not become less difficult. The contradiction is great. When we think of the Church we think of that society of which Christ is the Head and of which he inspires every part; when we think of the churches we think of organizations which have many different heads or principles—papacy and papal infallibility, bishops and apostolic succession, congregational authority, the Bible and literal inspiration, reason and rationality, liberal thought and aspiration after human welfare. We may and must call the churches Christian, but when we do so we mean that they are representatives in one way or another of that syncretistic thing, the Christian religion, rather than societies which derive their being from and represent Christ only.

There is a danger that in dwelling on these contradictions we forget the complementary factor—the close interrelation between Church and the churches. Antagonists of the latter are often surprised that, when they use the ammunition which reformers of the churches have supplied, these same reformers appear as the champions and defenders of the attacked societies. It is inevitable that this should be so, for in the churches the Church does seem to come to some sort of appearance and, what is more important, it seems that through the churches the greatest service can be rendered to the Church. To be sure, the claim of the churches to be the sole representatives of the Church on earth must be denied since often other societies appear as fairer representatives of the spirit of the Church than religious organizations do; the functionaries of the family, school, or state may minister more effectively in the manner of Christ than do the functionaries of the churches. Nevertheless, the presence of the Church is so tied up with the activity of the churches that we do not know how to separate them. How can the family be for us part of the Church if its life does not begin in and accompany the life of the churches? How shall friendship give us assurance of the presence of the Church if it does not possess the symbols and the common language of the churches? How shall we build and serve the Church without the prayers, works, and services of churches? It is through the churches that continuing testimony is borne to the limit of the human race in Christ, to the reality of reconciliation and forgiveness in the world, to the glory of our destiny in God. Through the conservatism of the churches there shines something of that infinite conservatism of the Church which seeks to save every life, physically and spiritually, and through their radicalism appears the great radicalism which challenges the absoluteness of every principle save that of loyalty to God. There is a grand intermixture of the conservatism of fear and of the radicalism of pride with this conservationism of the gospel and this intransigence of prophecy; but the Church and not only the world appears in the churches. Though the worship of the churches is shot through with self-worship, pride, and unconscious atheism, yet it remains as

almost our only reminder in the whole of our environment of the presence
beyond the veil of things of the one, transcendent, infinitely glorious and good
source and goal of all being. The preaching of the churches is often anxious,
defensive, and more secular than newspaper editorials; yet it cannot but contain echoes of the gospel of a Creator who is infinite love and of a salvation from
evil that is universal, eternal, and complete. The charity of the Church, confused though it may be with the demands of the institution and its functionaries for a share of the social wealth, yet proclaims the note of Christian
neighborliness and answers the question "Who is my neighbor?" as no other
society—class, family, or nation—can answer it. Where the cross is found, even
the red cross of warring nations, it is at least vaguely clear to men that every
man is neighbor to every other. It is unnecessary to multiply reminders of the
way in which the life of the churches is tied up with the Church. The fact is
clear. We do not know how to aspire after membership in the Church without
joining the churches nor how to build the holy Catholic society, the universal
fellowship of reconciliation, without increasing, reforming, supporting, and
even defending those contradictory organizations—our religious institutions,
these Western counterparts of Shintoist and Hindu cults.

II

Many efforts have been made to understand this paradoxical relationship and
to devise a corresponding strategy of action. The simplest solution of the problem will always have some vogue despite its absurdity. It is the solution which
is advanced by the Roman Church and by many another less powerful organization; doubtless we all tend to adopt it at times. It consists in identifying
one's own religious organization with the true Church and ascribing all the
contradictory features to other religious groups. So the Syllabus of Errors and
the decrees of the Vatican Council and the writings of many a Roman theologian, like the dithyrambic utterances of leaders of gospel tabernacles, assume
with ridiculous cocksureness that one's own religion and church is the true religion and true church and even that the particular organization in question has
the right to define what is true Church and what is not. What feats of self-
deception are necessary in order that one may ascribe the attributes of unity,
catholicity, holiness, and Christianity to an organization which one knows as
intimately as any priest or preacher knows his society is hard to guess. Perhaps
not many representatives of the churches are really deceived by these claims
and assertions; but they tend to maintain themselves in a state of intellectual
confusion in which the ridiculous nature of the claims does not become apparent. Yet it is evident that this solution of the problem of the Church and the

churches crops up again and again and leads to ever new foundations or institutions in which at long last the true Church is to be realized. A reading of the "autobiographical" sketches of religious groups in the U.S. Religious Census volumes indicates how recurrent and prevalent the error is. With respect to the unity of the Church, for instance, it is interesting and sad to read how many new splinter groups have been started for the sake of realizing the unity of the Church by founding a new and separated religious institution. So there is a group of churches of God which states that "to accept any specific title would imply that they are a sect, which they deny, sects or divisions being condemned" in Scriptures. Another organization states that its *distinctive* view is that "sectarianism is anti-Scriptural" while a third began its separate existence because it believed that "sects are unscriptural and unapostolic" and that "the sect name, spirit, and life should give place to the union and co-operation that distinguished the Church of the New Testament." Such statements as well as ideas prevalent in the churches in general point up another form of this common error—the belief that at some time in the past religious organizations truly represented the Church in its unity, holiness, and catholicity. Yet nothing is more evident from a reading of the New Testament than the fact that the empirical organizations of Christians in Jerusalem and in the days of Paul were shot through with strife and secularism. The error of explaining the relationship of the true Church to the churches by assigning the characteristics of the former to one of the empirical organizations is persistent and protean. Its persistence is doubtless due in part to our common sin of regarding our own kind of religious rite and organization as preferable to all others. It is due also to the inherent difficulty we encounter in separating the finite from the infinite. In any case this way of explaining the relation of the Church to the churches leads only to greater confusion in thought and action.

A second, frequently used way of dealing with this perennial problem is to assign the being of the Church to the realm of ideality while the churches are regarded as belonging to the realm of sense experience. A. C. Headlam in his book *The Doctrine of the Church and Christian Reunion* offers a clear-cut example of this mode of explanation. He writes, "Our explanation of the term 'one,' as applied to the Church, must be similar to that which we gave to the terms 'Holy,' 'Catholic,' and 'Apostolic.' It, like them, presents an ideal. When we say that the Church is 'one' we mean that Christ intended it to be 'one,' as he intended it to be 'holy.' . . . We must always have that ideal before us. Every step toward Christian unity makes Christianity fulfil its mission more perfectly."[1] The

---

1. Second edition (London: John Murray, 1921), p. 217. [Ed. note: ellipses are original to the essay.]

explanation is plausible so far as it goes. Within the Christian churches and within that great mass of religious movements which we call the Christian religion[,] men do feel the presence of imperatives to unite and to be holy and to make Christ their head. In this sense the one, holy Catholic Church is the ideal which is to be contrasted with the actual estate of the religious organizations. But the explanation does not help us very much. If in a somewhat Platonic sense it means that the empirical churches are imperfect, sensible representatives of an eternal reality, the difficulty is that the churches are not only imperfect but contradictory to the essence. If it means, as Dr. Headlam has it, that the one Catholic Church is the moral ideal in the minds of men associated in religious organizations[,] one must object that while this is true it is only a part of the truth. The difficulty is just this, that in the churches there are so many ideals besides the ideal of the Church. The ideal of the Roman Empire, more or less holy, haunts part of the religious movement called Christian; the ideal of Calvinist theocracy which was not so much theocracy as hierocracy is present in another part of that movement; the ideal of isolationism and of surcease of responsibility is always present in the sectarian sections of the churches. When unity is desired it is often wished for as a means to the end of greater power, as so many expressions about the need for church union today indicate. When holiness is praised as an end to be sought, it also is wanted because its presence would bestow greater influence on the churches. In all of this confusion there is no special indication that the one holy Catholic Church is the special ideal in the minds of the churches and churchmen. The principle is present without a doubt; it is strong enough to give men in the churches a bad conscience; but that it is the dominant ideal which directs their actions is contradicted by daily experience.

Another and more important consideration makes it difficult to accept this explanation of the relation of the Church to the churches. For Christians the only holy Catholic Church is not an ideal in the first place but an object of faith and love and an anchor of hope. It is an object of faith on which we rely as we do upon a friend, not as we depend—if ever we do depend—on an ideal in our mind or in a realm of essences. An ideal church depends on the churches for its realization; the Church of faith is more real and dependable than the churches; the latter are trustworthy only insofar as the former appears in them. This Church of faith is one in no ideal sense but in the real sense that it unites us with all our fellow men and that it unites all men in loyalty to the one God. It is one in the sense that it brings us into harmony and unity with the Creator and with Christ and with the Holy Spirit and that all these are present in it. To believe in the Catholic Church is to depend on the fact that nowhere upon earth and at no time shall we or our children or our neighbors be left without ministers of the grace of Christ and without witnesses to faith. It is a universal

Church[,] not as an ideal can be ubiquitous[,] but as a reality on which we count is universal. This Church is the society of those who never lose faith, never drop the flag of the world, never abandon their companions in the darkness. It is the holy company of those who receive a constant forgiveness and cleansing of their sins and who in measureless gratitude for measureless love forgive as they have been forgiven. It is the group of fellow workers in our time and in all times to come on which we rely to supplement and correct and remake our work so that it will be fit for eternity. It is the Christian Church of which Christ is the center, the brain, and the heart; he thinks in it and it feels as he does; his mind works in its searchings after truth and his self-forgetfulness inspires all its actions. Such a Church is not an ideal. It is not the sort of thing we can strive to bring into existence, for it is before us. This Church is our Mother. To think of it is to become aware anew of the painfulness of the contradiction in which our religious organizations stand to it. They are not imperfect beings tending to realize this character in their further development; they are beings of a different order of existence, more like wayward children than like the Mother.

There is one more explanation of the relation of the Church to the churches which must be considered. Protestantism, especially early Lutheranism, sought a solution for the problem with the aid of a formula ultimately derived from Augustine. There were two churches, it declared, a visible church and an invisible one; the invisible church is the Church of faith; the visible church is the human institution. But the relation of these two churches was never clearly worked out. Upon the one hand the contrast was used offensively to deny that the Roman Church with its high visibility was equivalent to the Church of faith; on the other hand, it was used defensively to maintain that the evangelical churches possessed the notes of the true Church: preaching of the gospel, rightful administration of the right sacraments, and discipline according to the Word of God. In part the distinction was one between the Church known only to God and the church known to men which is full of hypocrites and therefore not true; in part it was the distinction between the work of God and the work of men, since the invisible church is the company which God has chosen out of all times and places to be his holy people, while the visible church is the preachers' and elders' institution in which care must be taken that right doctrine is taught and right order prevails. Though the formula of the visible and invisible churches is suggestive it is also somewhat confusing. Insofar as it assumes that the Church of faith, the invisible company of the elect, is made up of scattered individuals, it seems to be in downright error, misconceiving the nature of society and of the Church in particular, which is not simply a society of saved men but the saved society of men.

III

Partly in continuation of this Protestant doctrine, but more upon the basis of biblical studies and of sociology of religion, it may be possible to formulate the outlines of a doctrine of the Church which will do ampler justice to the complex elements than the foregoing theories can do. Two ideas in particular seem to be called for in order to understand the situation: First, the Church is an eschatological society, or as we may better say in our times, it is an emergent reality, hidden yet real; and secondly, the religious institutions called the churches are subject like all the rest of this secular society of ours to a constant process of conversion; they are not the converted parts of society but the parts in which conversion makes its appearance in religious form.

The Church of faith is an eschatological society, that is to say, it belongs to that order of existence which can neither be described in temporal terms nor abstracted from the temporal. To say that Jesus is the Christ is to speak eschatologically. He is risen and yet he is not among us; he is the ever-present one who has come, yet we wait for his coming in glory and power, whether after the fashion of literalists or liberalists. Jesus Christ has come and all the world is different; Jesus Christ has not returned and the world is still lost in darkness; both statements are always made sooner or later by Christians. For they live between His first and second coming, in the revolutionary epoch of human existence when the old is passing but the new has not yet come into appearance. One cannot speak of Christ merely as an ideal though he is that; he is a Christ of faith on whom we rely as present power. Yet we say:

> O Son of man, to right my lot
>   Naught but thy presence can avail;
> Yet on the roads thy wheels are not
>   Nor on the seas thy sail.[2]

Likewise the Christian life itself is an emergent reality of which Christians must say with Paul that it "is hid with Christ in God," invisible to themselves and others, yet something to be counted upon. Is not the Church a reality of this order? It is the society which is at the very edge of coming into existence, more real than all the communities which are passing away; but it is not to be seen. It is an emergent as mind was an emergent through the long ages when it was the most powerful thing in the world but had not yet become conscious of itself and was in that sense invisible, being confused and confounded with

2. George MacDonald, "That Holy Thing," second stanza, in Arthur Quiller-Couch, ed., *The Oxford Book of English Verse 1250–1900* (Oxford: Clarendon Press, 1919), no. 710. [Ed.]

sense and the physical. The Church is the society of that new order of creation in which all things shall become and are new. We may say that that order has been coming into being for a few thousand years but that its outlines cannot yet be discerned, or we may say that the order so far transcends our present existence that we must speak of it as belonging to eternity rather than time. In any case what we mean is that we stand at the edge of the new and are so close to it that we count upon it. In one sense it is not yet at hand, but in another sense everything else has passed and only this new world of God with its Church of faith is real.

The revolutionary situation in which Christians stand requires many paradoxical statements for its description. It is not true that the revolution which makes all things new has not yet taken place and that men must wait to the end of time for the realization of the promises. But neither is it true that the revolution has taken place, that mankind has been reborn and that all things have been re-established in the glory intended by the Creator. These churches and states, these codes of morals and these creeds are not the institutions of the new world of God which are to be defended against all adversaries. They belong to the old life that is passing away, but no substitute forms of church or state, of moral code or creed, can take their place and be regarded as the institutions of the Christ. All these things are somehow of the same order and the Church which is emergent is of a new order and a new kind. Under the circumstances a double attitude is always called for and possible to Christians: an attitude of confidence and joy in the Church, an attitude of sorrow and repentance in their churches and for their churches.

A second item in a satisfactory theory of the Church is the idea of conversion. Conversion, or the turning of the mind and heart toward God in Christ, toward obedience and faith, is not so much the isolated event which some sorts of religion tend to make of it as a process which accompanies the whole of the Christian life. It is continuous and ever-renewed in view of the fact that we fall away again and again into anxiety and polytheism and atheism and in further view of the infirmity of the divine goodness toward which we are turned. Moreover, conversion is the very heart of the Christian faith, for it is the change of mind which the reception of the gospel of the Kingdom brings with it. Such conversion is antithetical to substitution. In the Christian life human *eros* is not supplanted by divine *agape* but the divine *agape* converts the human *eros* by directing it in gratitude toward God and toward the neighbor in God. The community of the family is not supplanted by a monastic society but the hearts of fathers and children and husbands and wives are turned toward each other in reconciliation because of the divine forgiveness. The gospel restores and converts and turns again; it does not destroy and rebuild by substituting one finite structure of life or thought for another. And this strategy of the gospel applies to the religious institutions and organizations of men. As Jewish synagogue and Roman basilica are changed into churches in a physical sense so the religious societies of men are subject to the long process of internal rebirth whereby they are turned from the little gods to the One beyond all gods, from despair to happy confidence and from defensiveness to loyal helpfulness of the brothers. Our Christian churches, so-called, are like ourselves, just human entities on which God has taken mercy and which he is converting to himself. In them and through them we sin and falter as we do in and through our families and our states. But in and through them we can serve the Church of our faith as we can nowhere else. The preaching of the gospel, the administering of the sacraments, and the provision of a decent order—these are not the signs of the presence of the great Mother of us all, the Church of God, but they are the duties we can perform in order to minister to that Church and to declare our faith in its presence.

Such reflections about the emergent nature of the true Church and about the continuous necessity of converting our religious organizations do not give us final satisfaction. They do not assuage the pain we feel as we contemplate the contradiction in our life. But since we live in hope and not by sight we learn a certain patience in this situation too and rejoice in the Church even while our tears fall for the churches and for ourselves as churchmen.

7

The Responsibility of the Church for Society [1946]

1. THE URGENCY OF THE QUESTION

The question of the Church's responsibility for the society in or with which it lives has been important and difficult since the beginning of Christian history. Neither Jesus nor his disciples found an easy answer to it. The Master was greatly concerned for the lost sheep of the house of Israel and loved Jerusalem with moving devotion. Yet his striking lack of interest in conserving the institutions and the culture of his society enables modern Jewish scholars such as Rabbi Klausner to maintain with some persuasiveness that the guardians of Jewish society were justified in rejecting his leadership. This apparently paradoxical attitude of the gospels is restated in variant forms in the other New Testament documents and in the writings of the Christian fathers. It is mirrored in the dual and antithetical types of Christian organization—the so-called "churches" which undertake to organize and defend the nations and cultures in which they function, and the so-called "sects" which withdraw from the world of non-Christian society.

Though the problem is so rooted in the nature of both Church and secular society that it is always present, yet it has a peculiar urgency for the modern church which is confronted with unusual evidences of misery in the life of human communities and of weakness within itself. Christians live today in and with nations that are either dying or over which the threat of doom hangs like a heavy cloud. Some of them are miserable in abject physical poverty; some seem hopelessly divided within themselves; some are powerful and affluent beyond the imagination of past years but full of internal anxieties and badgered by fears. In a general atmosphere of spiritual confusion political decisions are made uncertainly and hesitatingly. Apprehension of disaster has taken the place of the hope of progress as the dominant mood and motive of action.

Looking upon these societies, Christians, individually and in the community of the Church, are moved to weep over them as Jeremiah and Jesus wept over

Jerusalem. They feel impelled to seek the peace of the cities in which they dwell as Paul and Augustine sought the peace of Rome. Their sense of responsibility has many roots—the love of neighbor inculcated by centuries of teaching and example, the faith in a God whose nature it is to order and redeem no less than to create. But one highly important root of the sense of obligation is the Christians' recognition that they have done not a little to make the secular societies what they are. In this respect the modern church is in a wholly different position from that which the New Testament church or even the church of Augustine's time occupied. The Christian community of our time, whether or not formally united, is one of the great organizations and movements in civilization; it is one of the oldest human societies; it has been the teacher of most of the nations now in existence. It cannot compare itself with the small, weak company of the early centuries living in the midst of secular societies that had grown up independently of it. The American, Russian and British empires as well as the German and Italian, challenge the Church to a sense of responsibility, therefore, which the Roman Empire could never call forth. They were not suckled in their infancy by wolves but nursed and baptized by the Church; it instructed them in their youth and has been the companion of their maturity.

The poignancy and urgency of the present question about the Church's responsibility for society are due then as much to the Church's consideration of its own plight as to its sympathy with the tragic empires and threatened cities of our age. It is doubtful whether Christian communities have suffered more from bad conscience at any time since the sixteenth century than they do now. There have been times when the Church felt itself more seriously threatened from without than it does today, but it has not often questioned its own adequacy so much as it does now and a major cause of this self-questioning is its sense of responsibility for the ruined and threatened societies with which it is associated.

When these things are spoken of many voices offer many counsels. No single, clear, prophetic cry challenges the attention and consent of Christians in mass. Perhaps no such voice will be heard; not every time of crisis is blessed with the gift of an apostle or reformer. Christian people may need to find their way today, as in some past periods of confusion, by means of simple, democratic, equalitarian discussion and decision, relying on no dominant human leader but on the Spirit in the churches. However that may be, in anticipation or without hope of prophetic revival, the time requires of all Christian folk in all these associations profound and continuous thought on the great issues of human life. In particular they need to reflect upon their responsibility for the states, nations and cultures of mankind so that their social decisions may be made in the full light of understanding rather than under the guidance of ancient habit or of emotionally charged catchwords. The following reflections are offered as a contribution to that end. Beginning with a definition of the Christian idea of responsibility they proceed to examine the erroneous or heretical forms of church responsibility and conclude with an effort to understand the positive content of the Church's social obligation by considering its functions as apostle, pastor and pioneer of humanity.

2. THE MEANING OF CHRISTIAN RESPONSIBILITY

Responsibility To and For

To be responsible is to be able and required to give account *to* someone *for* something. The idea of responsibility, with the freedom and obligation it implies, has its place in the context of social relations. To be responsible is to be a self in the presence of other selves, to whom one is bound and to whom one is able to answer freely; responsibility includes stewardship or trusteeship over things that belong to the common life of the selves. The question about the one *to* whom account must be rendered is of equal importance with the question about the what *for* which one must answer. The responsibility of rulers in political society varies not only with the number of functions they exercise but also with the sovereign to whom they must account for their rulership. The doctrine of divine right makes kings responsible to God alone and exempts them from all obligation to answer to the people. An extreme type of democratic doctrine teaches that governors are responsible only to the people they govern or to the majority of such people. Most modern democracies rest on a profounder and less popular conception of responsibility, both rulers and people being regarded as accountable to some universal principle— God, Nature or Reason—as well as to one another. The difference between these two conceptions of democracy is very great. For the first kind, the will of the people is sovereign and makes anything right or wrong; the representatives of the people are bound to obey the popular desire. According to the second conception, there is a moral law to which the people themselves owe allegiance and which governors, legislatures and courts are bound to obey even in opposition to the popular will. Such a conception of responsibility is implicit in the Bill of Rights.

The Kinds of Irresponsibility

The double reference implied in the concept of responsibility is clarified by an examination of the nature of irresponsibility. A person may be irresponsible, of course, in the sense that he lacks the true qualifications of a self, but if he has freedom or the ability to answer he may be morally irresponsible in the sense that he refuses to give account to those to whom he owes an answer for common goods, or in the sense that he offers a false account for the things entrusted to him. The first sort of irresponsibility is the kind which appears in the "public-be-damned" attitude once explicitly adopted by some great corporations and still somewhat in vogue, as when great manufacturing or financial concerns resist the right of the public to be given an accounting for human and monetary values. The second sort of irresponsibility appears in the economic life in the criminal acts of defaulters who falsify accounts. Politically the first sort of irresponsibility is manifest in the claim of nations to sovereignty, that is, to their claim to be under obligation to no power beyond themselves or to be justified in doing anything that seems necessary to preserve national existence. The second type of irresponsibility in the political life may be found in wastage of natural resources and particularly in the political exploitation of human lives, in the name of some high ideal.

The Scope of Responsibility

It is clear from these examples and from reflection on ordinary experience that the "*to-whom*" and the "*for-what*" elements in responsibility are closely connected. What a man is responsible for depends in part at least on the being to whom he is accountable. If he must make answer to a nation he is required to consider more values than if he must answer only to the stockholders of a mercantile company. Some of the perennial conflicts between representatives of political and of economic institutions seem to be due to the fact that the former generally have future generations in mind, while the latter rarely have, whether they are labor leaders or businessmen. If a man responds to the demands of a universal God then the neighbors for whom he is responsible are not only the members of the nation to which he belongs but the members of the total society over which God presides. If one must give account to a God who tries the "heart and reins," then one must answer for invisible as well as for overt acts. Responsibility is a universal feature of the social life of men, but the content of responsibility varies with the nature of the society to which men understand themselves to belong. In the company of God and of immortal souls even family responsibility is greater and more inclusive than in the company of nations and of men who are regarded as purely temporal beings. When men know that they stand before an infinite judge and creator the content of their obligation becomes infinite; they are required to exercise moral freedom in all areas of existence; no part of conduct remains a matter of indifference or subject to pure necessity; nowhere can man act without the liberty and obligation of moral agency.

Responsibility to God

These reflections on the general nature of responsibility have partly defined the form of the Church's accountability. The Christian community must conceive its responsibility in terms of membership in the divine and universal society; it knows that it must give answer to the God who is Lord of heaven and earth for everything with which it deals. It is necessary, however, if the Church's peculiar sense of obligation is to be illuminated, to define the Being to whom it is answerable as *God-in-Christ* and *Christ-in-God*. Indeed the Church itself must be described in these terms as the community which responds to God-in-Christ and Christ-in-God. A society which does not acknowledge its obligation to render account to this God and this Christ may call itself church but it is difficult to attach specific meaning to the term. Without the sense of moral dependence upon or of obligation to Christ a society lacks the moral reality of the Church. It may be a religious association of some sort but it is no church in the historic sense of the word. In the New Testament the Church appears, first of all, as the company of those who answer the call of Jesus and then as the fellowship of those who await his return. In both instances the Church responds to more than a historical Jesus. The disciples answer him as one who has authority. He is a prophet and more than a prophet. He has words of eternal life. There is a universal and an everlasting, a powerful, inescapable content in what he says and does. When they respond to him and follow him they respond and follow an eternal reality in the temporal. In awaiting his return they anticipate the coming of no finite and passing being, but of one who represents the victory of life over death, of love over evil. Before his judgment seat they expect to be required to give account not for their treatment of the limited number of friends and neighbors of the finite Jesus, but of all the sick, imprisoned, hungry, thirsty men of the world—the neighbors, brothers and companions of an omnipresent being. It is to God-in-Christ, to the universal, absolute and unconditioned in the particular that the early church renders account. Moreover it feels its responsibility to God-in-Christ not only as an eschatological community hastening toward a final and inclusive judgment, but also as a spiritual society, aware of the presence of the living Spirit of Jesus Christ, which is the Spirit of God. At every moment the company of Christians as well as each Christian renders account to the present Lord who is in the midst of every two or three persons meeting in his name. Its responsibility is not merely a preparation to answer in the future for all its words and deeds, but a continuous opening of the whole book of life to the inspecting and correcting activity of the ever-present Spirit of God.

We must invert the formula now and note that the being to whom the Church responds is Christ-in-God as well as God-in-Christ. The Church looks not only to the absolute in the finite but to the redemptive principle in the absolute. God, it believes and confesses, is love; He is mercy; He so loved the world that He gave His best-loved for its redemption; it is His will that the wicked should not perish but turn from their ways and live. To be a Christian church is to be a community which is always aware of and always responding to the redemptive principle in the world, to Christ-in-God, to the Redeemer.

Universal Responsibility

It becomes clear that the content of the Church's responsibility is largely determined by the nature of the one to whom it renders account. Since it is God-in-Christ whom it answers the content of its responsibility is universal. It is not a corporation with limited liability. All beings existent in the world are the creatures of this creator and the concern of this redeemer. The questions, "Who is my neighbor?" and "What is good?" need to be answered in a wholly inclusive way by a Church which lives in the presence of and in expectation of the coming in power of this Lord. All men and all societies, all the realms of being, belong to the neighborhood in which this community of Christians is required to perform its functions for the common welfare. Whatever is, is good in the world of this God-in-Christ. It may be perverted, sinful, broken; but it is not bad, for God-in-Christ has made it and maintains it. Such universal responsibility is incompatible with a spiritualism that limits the Church's concern to immaterial values, with a moralism that does not understand the value of the sinner and the sinful nation, with an individualism that makes mankind as a whole and its societies of less concern to God than single persons, and with any of those particularistic and polytheistic theories of value and responsibility which substitute for God-in-Christ some other deity as the source of valuable being. Moreover, since it is Christ-in-God to whom account must be rendered the content of responsibility is always mercy. The Church is not responsible for the judgment or destruction of any beings in the world of God, but for the conservation, reformation, redemption and transfiguration of whatever creatures its action touches. Whatever may be said in terms of the eschatological parable about the future role of the Church as judge of the nations, nothing belongs to its present responsibility for which it cannot answer to the one who gave his life as ransom and whose whole activity was a seeking and saving of the lost.

3. IRRESPONSIBLE RELIGION

From this general description of the Church's responsibility we must now move to the consideration of its accountability for society. The nature of the latter may be illuminated for us to some extent if we consider, first of all, the ways in which the Church has been and can be socially irresponsible. Two sorts of temptations seem especially prevalent in history, the temptation to worldliness and the one to isolationism. In the case of the former the "*to whom*," in the case of the latter the "*for what*," of responsibility is mistakenly defined.

The Worldly Church

The first sort of irresponsibility or perversion of Christian social responsibility results from the substitution of human society itself for God-in-Christ. Instead of, "What doth the Lord require?" the question in the mind of the church which has fallen into this temptation is, "What does the nation or the civilization require?" It thinks of itself as responsible to society for God rather than to God for society. In this situation the church is more concerned about social approval and disapproval than about the divine judgment, and its end is more the promotion of the glory of society than of God. The societies to which Christians may feel responsible are various. Now it is a nation, now the society of mankind as a whole; now it is the conservative, now the radical or revolutionary part of the cultural group in which the church lives. Social religion in distinction from religion that is loyal to God-in-Christ is readily identifiable when the human unit whose glory it seeks is a nation, as in the case of that section of the church in Germany which equated the Christian cause with that of National Socialism. It is not as readily identifiable when the unit whose glory is to be promoted is mankind as a whole. Bergson, for instance, in his excellent discussion of *The Two Sources of Morality and Religion* notes that defensive religion is connected with closed societies, such as nations, but in relating the religion of aspiration to the open society of mankind as a whole he does not apparently note sufficiently that mankind as a whole is also finite. From the point of view of Christian faith a humanistic church is closely akin to a nationalistic church. The substitution of any society for the infinite and absolute God involves the Church in a kind of irresponsibility in the course of which it actually betrays the society it seeks to serve.

What is true of the difference between responsibility to the smaller or larger human society is true also of the difference between the sense of accountability to the more conservative and to the more revolutionary elements in society. Generally social religion of the sort described which depends on public approval seeks the esteem of those parts of society which have been established in power and enjoy the prestige attached to customary authority. The worldly church is usually a church which seeks to maintain the old order in society and with it the power of the monarchs and aristocrats, of the owners of property and of other vested rights. However, the temptation to worldliness arises also when a radical or revolutionary group seeks to seize power and when a church undertakes to gain the approval of such a group. The former temptation is great because of the Church's interest in order, the latter because of its interest in the reformation of unjust order, but in either case if it seeks to gain the good will simply of society or parts of society and makes itself responsible to them for supplying certain religious values it has become irresponsible in a Christian sense since it has substituted men for God. This sort of worldliness is a protean thing. It appears as feudalist, capitalist and proletarian Christianity, as nationalism and internationalism, as the defensive faith of the educated classes or as that of the untutored.

False Prophecy and False Priesthood

The church which has fallen into this temptation seeks to supply the societies upon whose approval it depends with supernatural grace or with religious aid of one sort or another. It tries to render account to men for its stewardship of religious values. It is a mediator of God not in the true prophetic sense but in the fashion of the false prophets. It tends to give society the assurance that its form of organization and its customs are divinely ordained, that it enjoys the special protection and favor of God, that it is a chosen people. Many Thanksgiving Day proclamations and sermons offer clear-cut examples of such pious worldliness. Again the secularized social church may undertake to aid a human society in its pursuit of the great values of peace and prosperity. It may do this by endeavoring to persuade men that the order which is in effect has divine sanction, by threatening all protests against it with supernatural punishment, and by scores of other more or less creditable devices. In ancient times and by non-Christian folk the usual method for gaining divine approval was by way of sacrifice. In more sophisticated times social religion may try to serve society by subjective and psychologically effective means, seeking to supply not so much a supernatural as a natural, psychological aid. It may try to generate "moral dynamic" by means of worship, assuage the passions with the aid of prayer and stimulate "good will" by means of meditation. It may turn its educational work into an effort to create "good citizens" or effective revolutionaries. The line between a Christian conduct that is responsible to God and one which is responsible to society is often hard to discover in such situations, but whenever worship has become subjective, that is, directed toward effecting socially desired changes in the worshiper, and education has become moralistic, it seems safe to assume that one is dealing with worldly religion.

The temptation to this sort of irresponsibility is particularly great in the modern world. It is great because human societies, in the form of nations and of civilizations, have become very powerful and seem to hold in their hands both the blessings and the curses that are to be visited on men. The belief that the fate of mankind depends on the decisions of the leaders of empire is widespread and pervasive. The temptation is enhanced by the long nurtured illusion of social progress, which leads men to believe that the meaning of human existence must be realized in some organization of human societies dwelling on the planet. Again the tendency to look upon all matters from a social point of view has increased the temptation of the Church to consider itself as responsible to society. Much social science, including the sociology of religion, has tended to erect society itself into a kind of first principle, the source of all human movements and institutions. It has not only described the relations of religion to other functions in social life but seemed to explain it as nothing but a social function. When the Church has accepted this view of itself it has given evidence of its complete fall into worldliness, for now it has substituted civilization or society for God as author and end of its being.

Isolationism in the Church

The most important reason, doubtless, for the prevalence of such "social religion" in modern Christian churches is their reaction against the isolationism which long characterized many of them. Isolationism is the heresy opposite to worldliness. It appears when the Church seeks to respond to God but does so only for itself. The isolated church is keenly aware of the fact that it must answer to God-in-Christ for all its deeds and for all the values it administers. But it thinks of itself as the being for which it must answer and it regards the secular societies with which it lives as outside the divine concern. Its attitude toward them is like that of certain Israelites toward the Gentiles or of Greeks toward barbarians—they are beyond the pale. What is required of the Church, according to this conception, is the intense development of its own life and the careful guarding of its holiness. This holiness religion is intensely self-regarding both with respect to the individual Christian and with respect to the Christian community. It thinks of the secular societies as antagonists of the Christian Church and as beyond the possibility of redemption. They are not only mortal but sinful and must be shunned so far as possible because contact with them is defiling. The Church, on the other hand, is the community of those who are to be saved from sin as well as death. It is the ark of salvation and the concern of its officers and crew is to see that it rides safely through the storms which bring destruction to other groups and other men.

It is not unfair to call this holiness religion irresponsible, for it is so in the definite sense that it disclaims accountability for secular societies. It rejects not only nationalism but nationality, not only worldliness but the world. The politics and economics and sometimes the family life of human groups are regarded by the extremer advocates of holiness faith as too defiling for contact. Hence the isolated church disclaims all interest in these social functions and with the disclaimer tends to abandon the secular societies to their own devices.

The history of the Church contains many examples of more or less extreme isolationism. Second-century Christianity, as represented in the epistles of John, in the *Didache* and other contemporary writings, tended to make the commandment not to love the world nor the things that are in the world into an injunction to separate the Christian community from the political and cultural societies of the time. It thought of the Church as a new society for the sake of which the world had been created and which was destined to govern the world. Again in the monastic movement the temptation to isolationism had to be combated ever and again by the great reformers who sought to make the monk a servant of mankind rather than a seeker after his own holiness. Protestant sects also have been tempted to pursue a sort of perfectionism that was highly self-regarding while another stream in Protestant religion has been so spiritualistic and individualistic that the concrete life of the secular societies has been actually ignored as beyond the scope of a spiritual church's responsibility.

These two sorts of irresponsibility, worldliness and isolationism, are evidently interdependent in so far as either extreme tends to call forth a reaction toward its antithesis. The general tendency of the Church in the twentieth century has been toward a conception of social responsibility which virtually made it an agent of secular society. Under the circumstances it is not impossible that a strong countermovement will arise and that Christians will seek forms of church life that are independent of secular society not only in source but also in purpose. The true measure of the Church's responsibility is not to be found, however, by attending to either extreme or by seeking for a compromise position between them but rather by attending to the two aspects of Christian responsibility in the right way. The relation to God and the relation to society must neither be confused with each other as is the case in social religion, nor separated from each other as is the case in Christian isolationism; they must be maintained in the unity of responsibility to God for the neighbor.

4. THE CHURCH AS APOSTLE, PASTOR AND PIONEER

The Church's responsibility to God for human societies doubtless varies with its own and the nations' changing positions, but it may be described in a general fashion by reference to the apostolic, the pastoral and the pioneering functions of the Christian community.

Apostolic Responsibility

The Church is by nature and commandment an apostolic community which exists for the sake of announcing the Gospel to all nations and of making them disciples of Christ. The function of the Church as apostolic messenger to individuals is clear-cut, but emphasis upon it ought not to lead to the obscuring of its mission to social groups. The Gospel must be announced in different fashion when it is addressed to America or to Russia from the way in which it is proclaimed to individual Americans or Russians. Here again no absolute distinction can be made but it does seem important and imperative that the Church should discharge its apostolic responsibility by envisaging the needs of men in their societies as well as in their isolation before God. This seems the more urgent in our time because the unbelief, the fear and sin of man come to exhibition more dramatically in the public life than elsewhere. The phenomenon of nationalism is religious in character; so also is the worship of civilization which seems to pervade the democratic societies. On the one hand, the social groups appear to be idolatrous in a sense that few of the individuals in them are; on the other hand, the idolatry of the great groups seems to arise out of that despair of God and the meaning of life for which the Gospel supplies the cure. As the apostolic Church it is the function of the Christian community to proclaim to the great human societies, with all the persuasiveness and imagination at its disposal, with all the skill it has in becoming all things to all men, that the center and heart of all things, the first and last Being, is utter goodness, complete love. It is the function of the Church to convince not only men but mankind, that the goodness which appeared in history in the form of Jesus Christ was not defeated but rose triumphantly from death. Today these messages are preached to individuals but their relevance to nations and civilizations is not adequately illuminated. The Church has not yet in its apostolic character made the transition from an individualistic to a social period which historic movements require. When it does take its social responsibility seriously it all too often thinks of society as a physical and not a spiritual form of human existence and it tends, therefore, to confine its care of society to interest in the prosperity and peace of men in their communities.

It is a part of the apostle's duty to continue the prophetic function of preaching repentance. The good news about the glory of divine goodness is neither rightly proclaimed nor rightly heard if it is not combined with the bad news about the great justice which prevails in God's world. It is impossible for the Church in Germany to give assurance to the German nation that it is not the will of God that this sinful people should perish without at the same time assuring the nation that its transgressions must be recognized and condemned. So the apostolic Church in America cannot announce the mercy of God without pointing out how this nation transgresses the limits assigned to men when it defrauds the Negro and refuses to condemn itself for the indiscriminate manner in which it made war in its use of obliteration bombing, or deals with defeated nations in the spirit of retribution rather than of redemption.

It is not enough that the Church should discharge its apostolic function by speaking to governments. Its message is to the nations and societies, not to the officials. A truly apostolic Church may indeed address presidents, legislatures, kings and dictators as the prophets and Paul did of old; but like them it will be less inclined to deal with the mighty than with the great mass, with the community as it exists among the humble. How the Church is to carry out this apostolic task in our time is one of the most difficult problems it confronts. Its habits and customs, its forms of speech and its methods of proclamation come from a time when individuals rather than societies were in the center of attention. Responsibility to the living God requires in this case as in all others an awareness of the immediate moment and its needs, a willingness to reconstruct one's own habits in order that the neighbor's needs may be met, a readiness to depart from tradition in order that the great tradition of service may be followed.

The Shepherd of the Lost

The Church discharges its responsibility to God for society in carrying out its pastoral as well as its apostolic functions. It responds to Christ-in-God by being a shepherd of the sheep, a seeker of the lost, the friend of publicans and sinners, of the poor and brokenhearted. Because of its pastoral interest in individuals the Church has found itself forced to take an interest in political and economic measures or institutions. Many of the early leaders of the social gospel movement were pastors whose concern for individual slum dwellers, the poor, the prisoners and the sick led them to attack the social sources of human misery and to understand the corporate character of human sin. Genuine pastoral interest in individuals will always lead to such results. The Church cannot be responsible to God for men without becoming responsible for their societies. As the interdependence of men increases in industrial and technological civilization the responsibility for dealing with the great networks of interrelationship increases. If the individual sheep is to be protected the flock must be guarded.

The pastoral responsibility of the Church for society is, however, direct as well as indirect. Compassion and concern for the Jewish people as a whole, pastoral interest in the defeated nations and in the victors who stand in great moral danger characterize the Church which responds to the God who not only creates men but also their societies. This pastoral mission of the Church to the nations includes all those measures of large-scale relief and liberation which the times call for. It cannot be sufficient for the Church to call upon the governments of nations to feed the hungry and clothe the naked. Direct action is required here as elsewhere.

The Church as Social Pioneer

Finally, the social responsibility of the Church needs to be described as that of the pioneer. The Church is that part of the human community which responds first to God-in-Christ and Christ-in-God. It is the sensitive and responsive part in every society and mankind as a whole. It is that group which hears the Word of God, which sees His judgments, which has the vision of the resurrection. In its relations with God it is the pioneer part of society that responds to God on behalf of the whole society, somewhat, we may say, as science is the pioneer in responding to pattern or rationality in experience and as artists are the pioneers in responding to beauty. This sort of social responsibility may be illustrated by reference to the Hebrew people and the prophetic remnant. The Israelites, as the major prophets ultimately came to see, had been chosen by God to lead all nations to Him. It was that part of the human race which pioneered in understanding the vanity of idol worship and in obeying the law of brother-love. Hence in it all nations were eventually to be blessed. The idea of representational responsibility is illustrated particularly by Jesus Christ. As has often been pointed out by theology, from New Testament times onward, he is the first-born of many brothers not only in resurrection but in rendering obedience to God. His obedience was a sort of pioneering and representative obedience; he obeyed on behalf of men, and so showed what men could do and drew forth a divine response in turn toward all the men he represented. He discerned the divine mercy and relied upon it as representing men and pioneering for them.

This thought of pioneering or representational responsibility has been somewhat obscured during the long centuries of individualist overemphasis. Its expression in the legal terms of traditional theology is strange and often meaningless to modern ears. Yet with our understanding of the way that life is involved with life, of the manner in which self and society are bound together, of the way in which small groups within a nation act for the whole, it seems that we must move toward a conception similar to the Hebraic and medieval one.

In this representational sense the Church is that part of human society, and that element in each particular society, which moves toward God, which as the priest acting for all men worships Him, which believes and trusts in Him on behalf of all, which is first to obey Him when it becomes aware of a new aspect of His will. Human society in all of its divisions and aspects does not believe. Its institutions are based on unbelief, on lack of confidence in the Lord of heaven and earth. But the Church has conceived faith in God and moves in the spirit of that trust as the hopeful and obedient part of society.

In ethics it is the first to repent for the sins of a society and it repents on behalf of all. When it becomes apparent that slavery is transgression of the divine commandment, then the Church repents of it, turns its back upon it, abolishes it within itself. It does this not as the holy community separate from the world but as the pioneer and representative. It repents for the sin of the whole society and leads in the social act of repentance. When the property institutions of society are subject to question because innocent suffering illuminates their antagonism to the will of God, then the Church undertakes to change its own use of these institutions and to lead society in their reformation. So also the Church becomes a pioneer and representative of society in the practice of equality before God, in the reformation of institutions of rulership, in the acceptance of mutual responsibility of individuals for one another.

In our time, with its dramatic revelations of the evils of nationalism, of racialism and of economic imperialism it is the evident responsibility of the Church to repudiate these attitudes within itself and to act as the pioneer of society in doing so. The apostolic proclamation of good and bad news to the colored races without a pioneering repudiation of racial discrimination in the Church contains a note of insincerity and unbelief. The prophetic denunciation of nationalism without a resolute rejection of nationalism in the Church is mostly rhetorical. As the representative and pioneer of mankind the Church meets its social responsibility when in its own thinking[,] organization and action it functions as a world society, undivided by race, class and national interests.

This seems to be the highest form of social responsibility in the Church. It is the direct demonstration of love of God and neighbor rather than a repetition of the commandment to self and others. It is the radical demonstration of faith. Where this responsibility is being exercised there is no longer any question about the reality of the Church. In pioneering and representative action of response to God in Christ the invisible Church becomes visible and the deed of Christ is reduplicated.

FURTHER READING

Brunner, Emil. *The Divine Imperative*. New York: The Macmillan Company, 1937.

Ehrenstrom, Nils, and Others. *Christian Faith and Common Life*. London: George Allen & Unwin, Ltd., 1938.

Niebuhr, Reinhold. *The Children of Light and the Children of Darkness*. New York: Charles Scribner's Sons, 1944.

Temple, William. *Christianity and the Social Order*. New York: Penguin Books, Inc., 1942.

Visser 't Hooft, W. A., and Oldham, J. H. *The Church and Its Function in Society*. Chicago: Willett, Clark & Company, 1937.

8

The Norm of the Church [1946]

The question about the norm of the church may be asked in at least three different ways. An observer and describer may seek to define what is and what is not church by means of certain criteria or characteristics which are the recognizable attributes of church. These constitute the norm of the church for him. Secondly, the church may ask about that principle which makes it the moral community it is and which could not be abandoned without self-destruction. This is the norm of the church in an ethical or existential sense. There is, in the third place, the familiar question about the notes or marks of the church. At first sight this seems to be the same question as the first one but when it is examined one discovers that there is a difference; the third question is raised within and by the church rather than by the disinterested observer and its meanings seem to be: Whom and what must we, as church, acknowledge as part of our community and whom and what must we reject if we are to remain true to our own being; and, further, how can we recognize what is part of the community and what is not? In the sequel we shall explore each of these approaches to our problem and ask about interrelations.

I

The first of the three questions is often regarded as fundamental in a time when empirical science dominates thinking and phenomena take value precedence over noumena. Whether or not it is fundamental, it is actual and may have some relevance to the other two questions. It is asked by sociologists—in our time especially by the sociologists of religion—by anthropologists and historians. When it is asked by members of the church they seek to take the standpoint of "disinterested" science, at least for the purpose of seeing themselves as others see them. The question of the norm may be raised by such observers first of all in the preliminary fashion of those who need to limit the scope of their inquiry and are required to define for themselves what they will and will not regard as church. Secondly, the question of the norm may be raised by them in the sense of an inquiry after what is essential in the nature of functioning of the organizations they are examining.

So far as preliminary definition is concerned, it is usual practice to delimit the church in two ways: first of all a religious institution or society needs to be distinguished from the non-religious; secondly, Christian institutions or societies are separated from the non-Christian. In general there seems to be wide agreement among observers and describers so far as this initial definition and its norm are concerned. What makes a church a church? H. Paul Douglass answers the question in this fashion in his article on "Church and Community in the United States": "Scientifically speaking, the inevitable marks of the church seem to be the following: It is a permanent grouping of people possessed of the 'we' sentiment in the field of religion, together with their reciprocating attitudes toward one another and the conventional behavior patterns which hold in this field. The church group also invariably has and holds in common certain cultural objects of symbolic value, highly charged with emotion and sentiment. It is a communion in holy things; for Christians, the Bible, the sacraments, the cross. The church group almost invariably also possesses cultural objects of utilitarian value. Its spiritual enterprises require material facilities so that it becomes a communion in real estate and buildings, as well as in holy things. . . . Finally, the church possesses language symbols, either oral or written, expressing rationalized patterns in the realms of thought and conduct. It has a creed and a code, whether or not formally expressed."[1] Other descriptions of a similar sort may be found in social surveys, sociologies, and histories.[2]

---

1. H. Paul Douglass, "Church and Community in the United States," in *Church and Community*, ed. Kenneth Scott Latourette, vol. 5 of the Church, Community and State series from the 1937 Oxford Conference on Life and Work (London: George Allen & Unwin, 1938), pp. 194–95. [Ed. note: This citation has been moved from within the text and expanded to include full bibliographic information.]

2. Cf. Joachim Wach, *Sociology of Religion* (Chicago: University of Chicago Press, 1944), pp. 141–45; H. Paul Douglass and Edmund de S. Brunner, *The Protestant Church as a Social Institution* (New York and London: Harper & Brothers, 1935), pp. 3ff.; Robert Staughton Lynd and Helen Merrell Lynd, *Middletown: A Study in Modern American Culture* (New York: Harcourt, Brace, 1929), part V; Talcott Parsons, *The Structure of Social Action: A Study in Social Theory with Reference to a Group of Recent European Writers* (New York and London: McGraw Hill, 1937); Charles Guignebert, *Christianity, Past and Present* (New York: Macmillan, 1927). [Authors' full names, book subtitles, and publishers' names have been added. Ed.]

The previously mentioned point about the external character of such definitions of the church is immediately apparent in the example given. The elaborate language Mr. Douglass employs is evidently the product of a resolute effort to look at the church wholly from the outside, to abstract from any knowledge that might have accrued to one from identification with the community, to speak about it with complete "objectivity." Hence it is plain that whenever the effort is made to describe the character of the church in this fashion all that can possibly be described is the character of the sensible phenomenon called church. (Whether or not this visible phenomenon is identical with the "visible church" is another matter.) A second characteristic of most and probably all such efforts to define what is and what is not church is the acceptance of the initial presupposition that church belongs to the order of religious institutions or communities. With this assumption one usually combines the idea that other institutions are not religious, or that religion is a specialized function of a person and of a society which enters into relations, more or less intelligible, with such other functions as education, economic activity, politics, etc. Thirdly, these efforts to define the church assume that there is a Christian religion which is of the general order of religion but in a specialized form. Finally, it is assumed that the so-called *concrete* community (Douglass' term) or *natural* community (a city, nation, civilization) is a thing-in-itself, while church or religious institution is dependent upon such a concrete community. The same assumption may be stated in another manner: the observer and describer is never independent of every community but he identifies himself with another community than the church when he regards, measures, and defines the church. As sociologist he may take the standpoint of a society of savants, but usually it is apparent that the standpoint is that of the culture community. The question is: What sort of an institution in the civilized community is the church?

The general or formal answer to the question when it is posed in this way runs about as follows: A church is a church when as a religious institution it provides for the practice of the Christian religion in a human group.

Now, of course, the real difficulty arises for the question has only been pushed back a step and the essence of religion and of Christian religion must be defined. What is the Christian religion and what is its norm? To this question innumerable answers can be given. Those who seek to maintain complete "objectivity" will look for sensible items of behavior which can be classified as Christian—because it is common usage to do so. A religious institution is a church when it uses the cross, the Bible, the name of Jesus Christ in its cult. Others, like Joachim Wach, posit a central religious experience, a subjective state, which varies in Christianity from the subjective religious state in other religions. They will look for the distinguishing mark of the psychological experience and classify that religious institution as a Christian church in which the external evidence indicates that a certain kind of religious experience prevails. Again the culture historian may seek by means of empathy so to enter into the spirit of Christian religious rites that he will be able to distinguish Christian religious practices from pagan, Jewish, or Hindu. But in the latter cases the standpoint of objectivity has been abandoned, at least temporarily. The norm is no longer objective and cannot be stated objectively; it must be "felt after." So long as we remain in the "scientific" attitude and look at the Christian religion as an object we cannot select some one criterion or group of criteria as constituting the essence of the Christian religion and the norm of its practice in the churches. Objectively regarded, the Christian religion is a great, syncretistic mass of beliefs, rites, codes, ideas, propositions, myths, forms of organization, patterns of thought and behavior which have been derived from many sources and which coalesce and separate again in a continuous kaleidoscopic movement.

From the beginning to end new societies and institutions arise; each is an historically individual event and Christian institutions are often difficult to distinguish from non-Christian. By arbitrary decision one may relegate to the ranks of the non-Christian all those institutions which show some trace of strange blood. But a truly radical procedure in this respect will leave us without any Christian churches at all. It remains within the rights of an observer and describer to draw his lines for the sake of convenience and to say that he will regard only those institutions as Christian in which some particular element is found. He is in his rights if he undertakes to describe the churches in which Jesus Christ is called Lord; or if he undertakes to study those institutions in which the Mass is celebrated, or the commandment of non-resistance is followed. But there is no single norm of the Christian religion which enables an observer to say that the religious institution which possesses the character described is "really" Christian.

II

The question about the norm of the church arises, secondly, in the moral or existential way. The church, beginning with itself and in itself, asks, "What must I become in order that I may be myself within my being?" Or, "What is the ideal in my real? What is the 'ought' within my being? What is the goal that corresponds to my existence and what [is] the imperative which I give myself as my own and inescapable law?" There are many ways in which the church asks the question but there is always one fundamental answer: Jesus Christ. Without loyalty to Jesus Christ the church is not church. Without the effort to incarnate his spirit it is not church but some other kind of community. The church's consciousness of belonging to Jesus Christ is as immediate as the self's awareness of itself. When we are in the presence of Jesus Christ we are church; when we are not in the presence of Jesus Christ our sense of being a "we" group may be ever so strong but we are not church and cannot know ourselves as the church, that is as the community which is the Lord's. To belong to the Lord and to be a church is in effect one and the same thing since no one can belong to the Lord alone. To be with the Lord is to be with those who mediate him (historical figures: "Matthew, Mark and Luke and John"; contemporaries, parents, teachers, etc.); it is to be with others with whom he is. The norm of the church is the presence of Jesus Christ. Psychologically or geographically, or in some other way, a community may begin with some other center than Jesus Christ and then become church, as when a family becomes church, or a nation does so, or a religious group which centers in awe of or fear of supernatural powers and then makes Jesus Christ its center. But logically the church begins with Jesus Christ and there is no logical transition from some other being to him. The church, therefore, is not primarily characterized by the fact that it is a religious community whose religion centers in Jesus Christ, but simply by the fact that as a community it centers in him. In some respects it is better to describe it from within as a moral rather than as a religious society, for its relation to Jesus Christ is not primarily one of worshipper and object of worship; its feelings about him are not necessarily first of all feelings of awe before a holy being. Another way of trying to say this is to call the roll of human associations and to say that each of them becomes and is church when Jesus Christ is its center. Family groups, workers' associations, schools, etc., may begin to ask themselves: What does Jesus Christ require of us? Then they are church; then they have raised the existential question of the church, whether or not they are in close contact with some religious institution.

This purely formal definition of the church's norm needs, of course, to be developed by the church in order that it may have specific knowledge of the nature and character of the one to whom it belongs and may know just what he promises and requires. This clarification of the mind of Christ and of the mind of the church, which with and in Christ legislates for and to itself, is a constant process going on throughout the life of the church. The church is Christian as it becomes Christian and it becomes Christian as it learns what the mind of Christ is. Its norm is the concrete mind of Christ and therefore the faith and the hope and the desire of Christ. In explicating this mind of Christ, the church sets forth its norm in the terms of confessions of faith and of codes of conduct. It knows that it does not belong to the Lord if it does not have his faith in the Father, his hope in the emergence of the power of the kingdom of God, his desire to seek and save the lost, to forgive the sins of men, to reconcile men to God and to one another. The norm of the church is stated in the theology and ethics of the community as well as in the confessions of faith which it uses as summaries. But since the person of Jesus Christ is the true norm of the church, no conceptualized statement of the content of his mind can ever take the place of the active intelligence and will. When a community substitutes for the person of Christ some set of metaphysical or legal propositions, it has begun to lose its character as church and to become a dogmatic or legal society.

In order that the church in its relation to Jesus Christ may distinguish between true and false spirits, or discern the difference between the spirit of Jesus Christ and other spirits[,] it is necessary for the community to make the Scriptures, with their presentation of the incarnate Lord, a constant companion. There is no possibility of finding in tradition or in the socially recognized religious organizations with their rites consistent and unchanging criteria by means of which what is and what is not in the mind of Jesus Christ may be determined. But in the Scriptures, with their presentation in the Old Testament of the faith of Jesus Christ and with their New Testament witness to the historic nature of the person, the church possesses a consistent and unchanging objective criterion of what is and what is not in accordance with his spirit. This is not to say that the Scriptures are the norm of the church, the "only guide to faith and practice." The spirit and the mind and the presence of Jesus Christ in the church is the norm. The Scriptures, however, enable the church to understand that mind, revealing the direction, the convictions, and the interests present in its operation. The Scriptures have other uses in the church since it is through the revelation mediated by Scriptures that the church is brought into being. At this point, however, we need to consider only this fact that as the church asks itself how it can be loyal to Jesus Christ and think with him and hope with him it needs to say to itself that it cannot be loyal without making the Scriptures a constant object of study. It must return again and again to the Jesus of history and to the history without which Jesus is unintelligible, to the law and the prophets, the apostles and the evangelists. As the church explicates its faith it becomes aware of the fact that its loyalty is not to the Jesus of history only, nor to the risen Christ alone, but to the eternal Son of God incarnate in Jesus. But whether or not it is clear about the nature of Christ who is its companion, in any case it cannot know the mind of this Christ without dependence on the historical Jesus and therefore on the Scriptures.

Jesus Christ, the faith of Jesus Christ, and the Scriptures constitute the norm of the church in such fashion that the one implies the other. This does not mean that loyalty to the Scriptures is on the same plane with loyalty to Jesus Christ, but the Scriptures cannot be rejected without rejecting Jesus Christ and Jesus Christ cannot be accepted without his faith.

III

The third question about the norm is the question asked within the church when decision must be reached as to the other groups with which a church is to have fellowship. It is the question about the extent of the church. As we have noted above, this questions turns into one about the marks of the church, since a community which centers in Jesus Christ is continuous with all communities that center in him and seeks to understand by what visible marks it can recognize its companions. On the other hand, in a world that is often hostile and sometimes seeks to use the church for alien ends it seems important that the church discover what communities which pretend to be church are really hostile to Jesus Christ. For the sake of inclusion as well as of exclusion it is desirable, if not absolutely necessary, for a church community to be able to distinguish other church communities or for the church to learn about its extent and its limits.

The question about the marks of the church seems to be like the question about the religious institutions but differs from it at a number of points. It is not the inquiry into the character of the visible religious organizations, but it proceeds from the invisible to the visible. Positing the presence of loyalty to Jesus Christ, it seeks for external and recognizable indications of that presence. There is no predilection here for religious institutions, for the church is not primarily a society of worshippers, though worship is an accompaniment or even presupposition of all its acts. The problem now is not what kind of a religious organization is church, but how the presence of a community of those who are loyal to Jesus Christ manifests itself.

It becomes clear as one seeks an answer to this question that no single mark or set of marks is to be associated with the presence of the church. None of the signs is infallible; all are subject to a variety of interpretations. It seems that one way in which the church of Jesus Christ would give evidence of its actuality would be through worship of the God of Jesus Christ. Where the faith of Jesus Christ is present there must be praise of the Father and dependence upon him; there must be intercession and petition. So once more, in an inverted way, the practice of religion comes to be regarded as a mark of the church and the practice of a peculiar kind of religion—one without idols, one that uses the prayers of Jesus Christ. But entirely too much attention may be paid by the Christian community to the presence of this mark. The community of Jesus Christ becomes apparent in an act of worship but not in an act of worship only—nor infallibly so nor primarily so. The act of Christian worship is not an infallible mark of the church since word and acts are always ambiguous and the presence which the rites and ceremonies of Christian religion manifest may be the presence of another being than the Lord. The phenomena of subjective worship are well known.

The Scriptures are a mark of the presence of the church since they are closely connected with Jesus Christ; but they are not an infallible mark since their appearance may indicate only the presence of faith in magic powers or of an Oriental society. Again the presence of order and discipline, apart from specific forms of order, is a mark of the church. But this is first of all true only in the negative sense that where there is no order, where there is evident anarchy and strife, there the church is not present since Jesus Christ is incompatible with disorder. If the test is applied positively, then it may be affirmed that where the church is present there an order of service must become apparent so that the highest are the servants of all. This test is also subject to misinterpretation and can be applied rigorously only in the negative form: where there is domination of man by man Jesus Christ is not present as the center of their relationship to each other.

Acts of charity, the giving of cups of cold water (by those who can afford no milk or wine), the healing of diseases, and above all, acts of forgiveness of the enemy and the seeking of the lost must rank as high as notes of the presence of the church as the traditional marks of correct rites and right order. Undue attention has been paid throughout the centuries to religious practices. The protests of the sects have been directed not only against the accommodation tendencies of the larger groups called churches, but also against the confusion of the Christian community, the church, with the Christian religion. The Reformation, despite its aid in overcoming the one-sided religious emphasis of medieval culture, still remained dependent on the conception of the church as religious institution and the revivals of the 18th century succeeded only in personalizing religion, not in reaffirming the community character of the church. The interest in that community as one which has other functions besides the religious has been kept alive to no small extent in the small sects and in some rather anti-religious societies.

The presence of the Christian church manifests itself, then, in no one single way but in a multitude of ways. There are more marks of the church's presence than there are of the presence of a person whom we may recognize by the sound of the voice, or of the footsteps, the shape of a hand, the use of a work, or any one of scores of symbols. There are no ways in which an infallible judgment may be made that Christian church is present. All that seems possible is a series of negative judgments, beginning with the apostolic test: If any man have not the spirit of Christ he is none of his. As in the case of the statement of the faith, so in the case of the marks of the church: one can proceed only with exclusions. The church takes for granted that all who profess loyalty to Christ are loyal and then excludes from that number those who show by their actions that they are not in the presence of Christ. Each period may need to set up a list of those particular confusions and fallacies which prevail in it. We can affirm today that where there is anti-Semitism the church is not present, that where nation is supreme there is no church, that where class conflict is proclaimed as the fundamental fact of human social existence the church is not at work. To set up a series of negative marks of the church's absence is unnecessary, however, as a matter of general principle; only crisis and the necessity of confessing loyalty to Jesus Christ by separating oneself from that which is contrary to his spirit justify the pronunciations of anathemas. For the rest the church does not need to know how great or small its extent is. It is after all a hidden church which works like yeast. The norm which is important for it is the existential norm and not the standard by means of which it might judge "those who are without."

9

The Church and Its Purpose [1956]

From The Purpose of the Church and Its Ministry, *Chapter 1*

TOWARD A DEFINITION OF THE CHURCH

. . . The results of the inquiry into the nature of the Church in which theologians and churchmen are engaged today cannot be anticipated.[1] The contributions on the one hand of Biblical, historical and systematic theology, of history, the sociology of religion and the theology of culture; and on the other, the practical experiments and experiences in ecumenical, national, municipal and parish organization of church life, will, one may hope, eventually be brought together in some kind of temporary historical synthesis. For the present the question what the Church is in act and potency, remains largely unanswered. The problem is new in many ways; at least it is posed in new forms at the present juncture of history. . . . In his effort to state tentatively and in his own way such apparently dawning agreements the author of this essay must employ the method of polar analysis; that is, he must try to do justice to the dynamic character of that social reality, the Church, by defining certain poles between which it moves or which it represents. Such a method is the best one available to him.

By Church, first of all, we mean the subjective pole of the objective rule of God. The Church is no more the kingdom of God than natural science is nature or written history the course of human events. It is the subject that apprehends its Object[2]; that thinks the Other; worships and depends on It;

1. Sections I and II of this chapter and parts of the first three paragraphs of this section, which mainly address theological education, have been omitted. [Ed.]

2. The objection that God is never object but always subject often arises from a confusion of the word "object" as meaning "thing" with "object" as meaning the Other toward which sensation, thought, appreciation, worship, et cetera are directed.

imitates It perhaps; sometimes reflects It; but is always distinct from its Object. It is integral to the self-consciousness of such a subject that it distinguishes itself from its Object. Several things are implied in this understanding of the Church: negatively, the Church is not the rule or realm of God; positively, there is no apprehension of the kingdom except in the Church; conversely, where there is apprehension of, and participation in, this Object there the Church exists; and, finally, the subject-counterpart of the kingdom is never an individual in isolation but one in community, that is, in the Church. Development of these themes would require more space than the scope of the present essay permits. What seems important is the distinction of the Church from the realm and rule of God; the recognition of the primacy and independence of the divine reality which can and does act without, beyond and often despite the Church; and the acceptance of the relativity yet indispensability of the Church in human relations to that reality.

Definition of subject and object are correlative. What the Church is as subject cannot be stated without some description of the Object toward which it is directed. Though an object is independent of a subject, yet it is inaccessible as it is in itself. What is accessible and knowable is so only from a certain point of view and in a certain relation. The communal point of view and perspective of the Church, or, better, the kind of receptivity created in the Church, puts it into a relation to its Object and makes possible an understanding of it that is impossible to every other point of view. The Church is not the only human community directed toward the divine reality; its uniqueness lies in its particular relation to that reality, a relation inseparable from Jesus Christ. It is related to God through Jesus Christ, first in the sense that Jesus Christ is the center of this community directed toward God; the Church takes its stand with Jesus Christ before God and knows him, though with many limitations, with the mind of Christ. Secondly, in that situation there is made available to it, or revealed to it, a characteristic and meaning in the Object—the divine reality—unknown from other perspectives, namely, the reconciling nature and activity of a God who is Father and Son, and also Holy Spirit. Once more it becomes evident that the effort to define the Church involves us in many problems of theology into which we cannot enter in this connection. But certain implications of the historic and apparently necessary Trinitarian understanding of the divine reality on which the Church depends may be called to attention as important for the reorientation of theological education. One of these implications is that in the relative situation occupied by the Church its function is always that of directing attention to its Object rather than to itself. Another is the recognition that it is inadequate and misleading to define the church and the Object on which it depends in terms of Jesus Christ alone. It is indeed the Christian Church, but as the Church of Jesus Christ it is primarily a Church of God and so related to, while distinguished from, all other communities related to the Ultimate.

We need to define Church further by use of the polar terms "community" and "institution." A social reality such as the Church cannot be described by means of one of these categories only and much misconception of the Church results from such exclusive use. Popularly and even among churchmen the institutional Church may be so emphasized that there is little appreciation for the Church that does not come to appearance in organizations and rites. Of the two ecumenical movements in our time the organizational effort to develop world-wide institutions takes precedence in many minds over that spiritual, psychological, intellectual and moral common life, transcending all national boundaries, which seeks institutions through which to express itself. Or again membership in the Church is widely regarded primarily as a matter of participation in institutional forms and actions, less frequently as engagement in common thought, common devotion and worship, common appreciations. But the opposite error is also possible; a common life, vaguely defined by reference to a common spirit also vaguely described, is exalted at the expense of institutional forms.[3]

These errors are like those made when a nation is defined either institutionally as state, or as pure community by reference only to national "spirit" or a "way of life." But it seems clear that no community can exist without some institutions that give it form, boundaries, discipline, and the possibilities of expression and common action. On the other hand, no institution can long exist without some common mind and drive that expresses and defines itself in institutions. The questions whether Church is primarily institution or primarily community, or whether one of these is prior, are as unanswerable as similar questions about thought and language. There is no thought without language and no language without thought, yet thought is not language nor language thought. The Church as institution can preserve as well as corrupt the Church as community; it can express and define through word and deed the common mind as well as thwart the common spirit. The Church as community can enliven but also stultify the Church as institution. So it was in the

---

3. An example of this may be found in Professor Emil Brunner's *The Misunderstanding of the Church* (Philadelphia[: Westminster Press], 1953). Professor Brunner writes: "The New Testament *Ecclesia*, the fellowship of Jesus Christ, is a pure communion of persons and has nothing of the character of an institution about it" (p. 17); to this "*Ecclesia* which is always . . . a dynamic reality and nothing more, the existing churchly institutions are related as means, . . . *externa subsidia*—in very diverse ways and proportions" (p. 109). "The *Ecclesia* . . . is no institution. Therefore the church can never be the *Ecclesia* either by purification or re-creation" (p. 107). [Ellipses were original to Niebuhr's text. Ed.]

case of the Nazi Christian community which twisted the meaning and eventually the forms of common Christian institutions; so it is also in the confusions of the Christian with the democratic community. The American and Canadian Church scene that we have sketched indicates how much institution and community belong together, yet how distinct they are. In part the realization of the Church community in the New World waits on the development of institutions able to give it form and wholeness; in part the institutionalization in denominations expresses the variety and unity characteristic of the community on this part of the planet.

To describe the Church as a community of memory and hope, sharing in the common memory not only of Jesus Christ but also of the mighty deeds of God known by Israel, expecting the coming into full view of the kingdom on earth and/or in heaven; to describe it further as the community of worship, united by its direction toward one God, who is Father, Son and Holy Spirit yet worshiped more as Father or as Son or as Holy Spirit in this or that part of the community; to describe it as a community of thought in which debate and conflict can take place because there is a fundamental frame of agreement and because there are common issues of great import—to do all this and the much more that needs to be done would be to essay the work of a large part of theology. It must be sufficient here to note that the schools which serve *in* the Church and serve the Church cannot abstract community from institution nor institution from community; nor can any churchman. One or the other of these polar characteristics of the social reality may be emphasized, but it cannot be defined without some reference to the other pole or served without some concern for its counterpart.

We must deal more briefly with certain other polarities in the Church's existence. Among these are the complementary yet antithetical characteristics of unity and plurality, of locality and universality, of protestant and catholic. The Church is one, yet also many. It is a pluralism moving toward unity and a unity diversifying and specifying itself. It is, in the inescapable New Testament figure, a body with many members none of which is the whole in miniature but in each of which the whole is symbolized. Every national church, every denomination, every local church, every temporal church order, can call itself Church by virtue of its participation in the whole; yet every one is only a member needing all the others in order to be truly itself and in order to participate in the whole. Without the members there is no body; without the body no members. Schools cannot prepare men to work simply in the whole Church but must equip them for particular service; yet they cannot do so unless they keep them mindful of the whole and loyal to it.

The Church is local and it is universal. Where two or three are gathered in the name of Christ there he is present, but all to which he points and all that he incarnates is present also. Among other things the universal Church is present, for Jesus Christ cannot be there without bringing with him the whole company of his brothers, who have heard the Word of God and kept it, who were not created without the Word. He is never present without the company of the apostles and prophets, the patriarchs and singers who speak of him; nor without the least of his brothers of whom he speaks. The localized Church implies the universal, but the universal no less implies the local; without localization, without becoming concrete in a specific occasion, it does not exist. The school which educates men for service in this Church cannot but focus their attention on the parish and the meeting; it cannot make them aware of the significance of parish or Sunday morning service unless it turns from the localized occasion to the universal community represented and adumbrated in the occasion.

The Church is protestant and catholic. This is not only to say that there is much historic Protestantism in those institutions called Catholic churches, and much historic Catholicism in the institutions called Protestant. It is also to say that the principle of protest against every tendency to confuse the symbol with what it symbolizes and the subject with the object, is a constituent element in the being of the community, even apart from the institutional organizations. The Church as the people of God, whether under the Old or the New Covenants, is always the party of protest against religion in the religious human world. It protests against every effort to bring the Infinite into the finite, the Transcendent into the immanent, the Eternal into the temporal. The only finite symbol of God it tolerates is the symbol of emptiness—the empty Holy of Holies, the empty tomb. But protest has no meaning apart from what is protested against. The Church cannot be protestant without being catholic. The principle of catholicity—as the principle of incarnation rather than the principle of universality—is as much an ingredient of churchliness as is the principle of protest. Unless the Infinite is represented in finite form, unless the Word becomes flesh over and over again, though only as oral preaching, unless the risen Christ manifests himself in the visible forms of individual saintliness and communal authority there is no human relation to the Infinite and Transcendent. Negative and positive movements—the one in rejection of all that is little because God is great, the other in affirmation of the apparently insignificant because God is its creator, redeemer and inspirer; the one away from the world that is not God, the other toward the world of which he is Lord—must both be represented where the Church exists.

The final polarity to be considered in this adumbration of the form and nature of the Church is that of Church and world. This is like the first polarity of subject and object insofar as it is not a polarity in the Church but one in which it participates as itself a kind of pole. The Church lives and defines itself in action vis-à-vis the world. World, however, is not object of Church as God is. World, rather, is companion of the Church, a community something like itself with which it lives before God. The world is sometimes enemy, sometimes partner of Church, often antagonist, always one to be befriended; now it is the co-knower, now the one that does not know what Church knows, now the knower of what Church does not know. The world is the community of those before God who feel rejected by God and reject him; again it is the community of those who do not know God and seem not to be known by him; or, it is the community of those who knowing God do not worship him. In all cases it is the community to which the Church addresses itself with its gospel, to which it gives an account of what it has seen and heard in divine revelation, which it invites to come and see and hear. The world is the community to which Christ comes and to which he sends his disciples. On the other hand, the world is the community of those who are occupied with temporal things. When, in its sense of rejection, it is preoccupied with these temporal matters it is the world of idolatry and becomes foe of the Church. When it is occupied with them as gifts of God—whether or not the consciousness of grace becomes explicit—it is the partner of the Church, doing what the Church, concerned with the nontemporal, cannot do; knowing what Church as such cannot know. Thus and in other ways the relations of Church and world are infinitely variable; but they are always dynamic and important. To train men for the ministry of the Church is to train them for ministry to the world and to introduce them to the conversation of Church and world, a conversation in which both humility and self-assurance have their proper place.

If our interpretation of the spirit of the Protestant theological schools is in any way correct then it is Church defined somewhat in the foregoing manner that constitutes the society in which they function and whose objectives they serve directly and indirectly, consciously or unconsciously. Different schools and different denominations doubtless represent different perspectives and emphases in their understanding of this Church; yet they participate in the common life insofar as they respect and gain profit from each other's contributions.

THE PURPOSE OF THE CHURCH: THE INCREASE OF THE LOVE OF GOD AND NEIGHBOR

What are the objectives of the Church? That they are many in number is clear from the statements of purpose made by schools when they define to what end they are training ministers, and by other church organizations—denominations, councils, conferences, et cetera—when they justify their activities. Some speak in individual terms of the cultivation of the Christian life or the salvation of souls; others state their goal to be the building up of the corporate life of the Church or of some part of it; again the goal is defined as the "communication of the vital and redeeming doctrines of Scriptures," or it is otherwise described by reference to the Bible as the ultimate source of all that is to be taught and preached. Elsewhere the end is defined as the preaching of the gospel and the administration of the sacraments; or, again, as the development of the life of prayer and worship. Perhaps most frequently the goal set forth is increase of belief in Jesus Christ, of discipleship to him and the glorification of his name. These multiple aims of churches and schools are again multiplied as one proceeds from grand statements about the purpose of the large organizations to the specialized goals of boards and departments, of courses and classes, of rural and urban congregations, of ministries of preaching and education and pastoral work and of preparation for such particular functions. The multiplicity of goals corresponds to the pluralism in the Church that is made up of many members, each with its own function; that stands in many relations to God, who is complex in his unity, and in many relations to a world protean in its attitudes toward God and the Church.

The question is whether there is one end beyond the many objectives as there is one Church in the many churches. Is there one goal to which all other goals are subordinate, not necessarily as means to end, but as proximate objectives that should be sought only in relation to a final purpose? When we deal with the complex activities of a biological organism or a person or a society the analogies of mechanical operation are misleading. The circulation of the blood, for instance, is not a means to the end of the functioning of the nervous system, nor is either a means only to the health of the body since that health also comes to expression in them. Still the healthy functioning of the whole body is in a sense a goal that a physician will have in view as he pursues the proximate end of improving circulation. The question of the ultimate objective of the whole Church and of the seminaries in the Church does not reduce questions about proximate ends to questions about means, but it poses the problem of the final unifying consideration that modifies all the special strivings.

Once more then we must venture to anticipate, though only in adumbrations, the answer to a question properly answerable only by the combined and continuous work of many theologians approaching the problem with the aid of many special studies and of many experiences. Such a statement will inevitably be somewhat private, yet though personal it is the report of what has been heard and understood in a conversation in which many contemporary ministers and teachers, many churchmen of the past and, above all, the prophets and apostles participate. As such a report it may gain some assent together with much correction and may be of some aid in moving forward the debate about the objective of the churches and their schools and in overcoming some current confusions.

The conversation about the ultimate objective is many faceted. It includes many interchanges on special issues through which, however, the movement toward the definition of the ultimate issue and the final objective proceeds. There is, as we have noted, a debate between those who define the last end of the Church individualistically as salvation of souls and those who think of it as the realization of the redeemed society. But extreme individualism and extreme emphasis on society are rare. Recognition of the social character of the individual and of the interpersonal character of society brings the parties somewhat closer to each other and both are challenged by the question: What is the chief end of man, whether as redeemed individual or redeemed community? Another debate, the one about Church and Bible, is leading, it appears, to somewhat similar results. Protestantism in general and particularly in America is marked by devotion to the Bible; it often conceives its end to be the dissemination of Biblical truth and increase of devotion to Scriptures. Catholicism, on the other hand, tends to be church-centered and often finds its goal in the building and strengthening of loyalty to the Church. But the study of the Bible in Protestantism, with its demonstrations of the close relations of the people and the Book both in the Old and New Covenant periods, and historical theology with its reflections on the manner in which at different times the Church interprets Bible, bring Church and Scriptures into inseparable relations of mutual dependence. Moreover, in practice concentration on the Book is ultimately self-corrective since the Bible faithfully studied allows none to make it the highest good or its glorification the final end. It always points beyond itself not so much to its associate, the people, as to the Creator, the suffering and risen Lord and the Inspirer. This is true also of the Church; it loses its character as Church when it concentrates on itself, worships itself and seeks to make love of Church the first commandment. Tension and antagonism between Bible-centered and Church-centered members of the community is being ever-renewed but is also being evermore resolved and their debate is led to higher issues by the witness of the Bible and the Church themselves to that which transcends both. Another long debate has gone on in history and is alive today among those who agree that the chief end of the Church is to gain followers of Jesus Christ or to proclaim his Lordship. Christian humanism, present to a minor extent in denominations and schools, but widely prevalent in the "latent" church which seems large and important in America, is strong in its devotion to the Son of Man; reliance upon the Son of God is more characteristic of the ecclesiastical institutions and of the majority movement in the community. Yet exclusively Jesus-centered and exclusively Christ-centered groups contradict not only each other but also contradict Jesus Christ himself who will not bear witness to himself but to the one who sent him. The great central position of the historic Church maintains itself amidst these variations, affirming not only the actuality and unity of both human and

divine natures, the identity of the historic with the risen Lord, but also some
form of the Trinitarian conviction, which does not allow the separation of the
Son of Man and Son of God, from the Father and the Spirit. Devotion directed
toward Jesus Christ is at least partly redirected by him to the One he loves and
who loves him, and to the world created and redeemed by the love of God.
Nothing less than God—albeit God in the mystery of his being as Father, Son
and Holy Spirit—is the object toward which Scriptures, Church and Jesus Christ
himself direct those who begin by loving them.

Is not the result of all these debates and the content of the confessions or
commandments of all these authorities this: that no substitute can be found
for the definition of the goal of the Church as the *increase among men of the love
of God and neighbor*? The terms vary; now the symbolic phrase is reconciliation
to God and man, now increase of gratitude for the forgiveness of sin, now the
realization of the kingdom or the coming of the Spirit, now the acceptance of
the gospel. But the simple language of Jesus Christ himself furnishes to most
Christians the most intelligible key to his own purpose and to that of the community gathered around him. If the increase among men of love of God and
neighbor is the ultimate objective may it not be that many of our confusions
and conflicts in churches and seminaries are due to failure to keep this goal in
view while we are busy in the pursuit of proximate ends that are indeed important, but which set us at cross-purposes when followed without adequate reference to the final good?

Any adequate discussion of the theme of love of God and neighbor and of
its relevance to Church and school requires all the resources of the theological
curriculum from study of the Scriptures through systematic theology, the philosophy, psychology and history of religion, Christian and social ethics to pastoral theology, Christian education and homiletics. Yet in relative brevity some
things can be said about this theme which, one hopes, will invite the assent of
many members of the community, however great their dissent because of the
incompleteness of the statement and because differences of emphasis are
inevitable. The statement of a final end can never be a final statement until the
whole community confesses it in the moment of its achievement.

In the language of Christianity love of God and neighbor is both "law" and
"gospel"; it is both the requirement laid on man by the Determiner of all things
and the gift given, albeit in incompleteness, by the self-giving of the Beloved.
It is the demand inscribed into infinitely aspiring human nature by the Creator;
its perversion in idolatry, hostility and self-centeredness is the heart of man's
tragedy; its reconstruction, redirection and empowerment is redemption from
evil. Love of God and neighbor is the gift given through Jesus Christ by the
demonstration in incarnation, words, deeds, death and resurrection that God
is love—a demonstration we but poorly apprehend yet sufficiently discern to

be moved to a faltering response of reciprocal love. The purpose of the gospel is not simply that we should believe in the love of God; it is that we should love him and neighbor. Faith in God's love toward man is perfected in man's love to God and neighbor. We love in incompleteness, not as redeemed but in the time of redemption, not in attainment but in hope. Through Jesus Christ we receive enough faith in God's love toward us to see at least the need for and the possibility of a responsive love on our part. We know enough of the possibility of love to God on our part to long for its perfection; we see enough of the reality of God's love toward us and neighbor to hope for its full revelation and so for our full response.

In both law and gospel the love of God and the love of neighbor are inseparably related. Historically they are associated in Judaism and Christianity, in the two tables of the Ten Commandments, in the double summary of the law offered by Jesus, in apostolic preaching, in the theology and ethics of Catholic and Protestant churches. Despite tendencies in Christian history toward solitary union with God on the one hand and toward nontheistic humanitarianism on the other the unity of the two motifs has been vindicated many times. The inseparability of the two loves has been less manifest in theological analysis than in the actuality of history but theology has pointed out often enough how the thought of God is impossible without thought of the neighbor and how the meaning and value of the companion's life depends on his relation to God. With their understanding of the divine-human nature of Jesus Christ and of the ubiquity of Christ in all compassionate and needy companions, Christians are led to see that as the neighbor cannot exist or be known or be valued without the existence, knowledge and love of God, so also God does not exist as God-for-us or become known or loved as God except in his and our relation to the neighbor. The interrelations of self, companion and God are so intricate that no member of this triad exists in his true nature without the others, nor can he be known or loved without the others. If we substitute "Jesus Christ" for "neighbor" Christians in general will accept that statement; but there is danger in that substitution as well as the possibility of enlightenment, since the relation of Jesus Christ to our other neighbors is often obscured in theology; his revelation of what it means to be a man is often forgotten in favor of exclusive attention to his disclosure of what it means that God is, and is Good. Yet the latter illumination could not take place without the former.

God's love of self and neighbor, neighbor's love of God and self, self's love of God and neighbor are so closely interrelated that none of the relations exists without the others. The intricacy and unity of the human situation before God is not less dynamic and complex than the one we encounter in nature when we explore the energetic world of the atom or of a sidereal system. Yet we can only speak in succession of what appears in contemporaneousness; in discourse we must abstract relations, such as love, from the terms related and the terms from each other, so that we are always in danger of speaking of God without reference to the being he loves and that loves him; of speaking about religion or love of God as distinct from ethics or the love of neighbor. Such dangers must be accepted and faced; theology must be content to spend no small part of its energies in the correction of the errors which ensue from its necessary mode of working.

What then is *love* and what do we mean by *God* and by *neighbor* when we speak of the ultimate purpose of Church, and so of theological education, as the increase of love of God and neighbor among men? By love we mean at least these attitudes and actions: rejoicing in the presence of the beloved, gratitude, reverence and loyalty toward him. Love is rejoicing over the existence of the beloved one; it is the desire that he be rather than not be; it is longing for his presence when he is absent; it is happiness in the thought of him; it is profound satisfaction over everything that makes him great and glorious. Love is gratitude: it is thankfulness for the existence of the beloved; it is the happy acceptance of everything that he gives without the jealous feeling that the self ought to be able to do as much; it is a gratitude that does not seek equality; it is wonder over the other's gift of himself in companionship. Love is reverence: it keeps its distance even as it draws near; it does not seek to absorb the other in the self or want to be absorbed by it; it rejoices in the otherness of the other; it desires the beloved to be what he is and does not seek to refashion him into a replica of the self or to make him a means to the self's advancement. As reverence love is and seeks knowledge of the other, not by way of curiosity nor for the sake of gaining power but in rejoicing and in wonder. In all such love there is an element of that "holy fear" which is not a form of flight but rather deep respect for the otherness of the beloved and the profound unwillingness to violate his integrity. Love is loyalty; it is the willingness to let the self be destroyed rather than that the other cease to be; it is the commitment of the self by self-binding will to make the other great. It is loyalty, too, to the other's cause—to his loyalty. As there is no patriotism where only the country is loved and not the country's cause—that for the sake of which the nation exists—so there is no love of God where God's cause is not loved, that which God loves and to which he has bound himself in sovereign freedom.

What, further, do we mean by the word God when we speak of the love of God? Not less than this surely—the Source and Center of all being, the Determiner of destiny, the Universal One—God the Father Almighty, Maker of Heaven and Earth. By God we cannot mean first of all love itself as the relation that binds all things together; the proposition that God is love cannot be converted without loss and error into the statement that love is God. Neither do we mean by God any lovely being easily made the object of our affection. We encounter no demand in ourselves or in our world to love that to which we are naturally attracted. Neither is there any promise or hope in the idea that we shall come to love with rejoicing, gratitude, reverence and loyalty, all that now easily arouses in us the movements of our desire. The movement of our love toward all these things, though they go by the name of God or gods, is the way of our idolatry; it is the movement toward the many away from the One, toward the partial instead of the universal, toward the work of our hands rather than toward our Maker. The demand and the promise refer to the One beyond all these.

The problem of man is how to love the One on whom he is completely, absolutely dependent; who is the Mystery behind the mystery of human existence in the fatefulness of its selfhood, of being this man among these men, in this time and all time, in the thus and so-ness of the strange actual world. It is the problem of reconciliation to the One from whom death proceeds as well as life, who makes demands too hard to bear, who sets us in the world where our beloved neighbors are the objects of seeming animosity, who appears as God of wrath as well as God of love. It is the problem that arises in its acutest form when life itself becomes a problem, when the goodness of existence is questionable, as it has been for most men at most times; when the ancient and universal suspicion arises that he is happiest who was never born and he next fortunate who died young.

Reconciliation to God is reconciliation to life itself; love to the Creator is love of being, rejoicing in existence, in its source, totality and particularity. Love to God is more than that, however, great as this demand and promise are. It is loyalty to the idea of God when the actuality of God is mystery; it is the affirmation of a universe and the devoted will to maintain a universal community at whatever cost to the self. It is the patriotism of the universal commonwealth, the kingdom of God, as a commonwealth of justice and love, the reality of which is sure to become evident. There is in such love of God a will-to-believe as the will-to-be-loyal to everything God and his kingdom stand for. Love to God is conviction that there is faithfulness at the heart of things: unity, reason, form and meaning in the plurality of being. It is the accompanying will to maintain or assert that unity, form and reason despite all appearances. The dark shadow of this love is our combative human loyalty which in its love of gods—principles of religion, empires and civilizations, and all partial things— denies while it seeks to affirm the ultimate loyalty and so involves us in apparently never-ending religious animosities which at the same time unite and divide neighbors, as they forge close bonds of loyalty to each other in a common cause among closed societies disloyal to each other.

Who, finally, is my *neighbor*, the companion whom I am commanded to love as myself or as I have been loved by my most loyal neighbor, the companion whose love is also promised me as mine is promised him? He is the near one and the far one; the one beside the road I travel here and now; the one removed from me by distances in time and space, in convictions and loyalties. He is my friend, the one who has shown compassion toward me; and my enemy, who fights against me. He is the one in need, in whose hunger, nakedness, imprisonment and illness I see or ought to see the universal suffering servant. He is the oppressed one who has not risen in rebellion against my oppression nor rewarded me according to my deserts as individual or member of a heedlessly exploiting group. He is the compassionate one who ministers to my needs: the stranger who takes me in; the father and mother, sister and brother. In him the image of the universal redeemer is seen as in a glass darkly. Christ is my neighbor, but the Christ in my neighbor is not Jesus; it is rather the eternal son of God incarnate in Jesus, revealed in Jesus Christ. The neighbor is in past and present and future, yet he is not simply mankind in its totality but rather in its articulation, the community of individuals and individuals in community. He is Augustine in the Roman Catholic Church and Socrates in Athens, and the Russian people, and the unborn generations who will bear the consequences of our failures, future persons for whom we are administering the entrusted wealth of nature and other greater common gifts. He is man and he is angel and he is animal and inorganic being, all that participates in being. That we ought to love these neighbors with rejoicing and with reverence, with gratitude and with loyalty is the demand we dimly recognize in our purer moments in science and religion, in art and politics. That we shall love them as we do not now, that is the hope which is too good to be true. That we are beloved by them and by God, that is the small faith, less than the mustard seed in size, which since the time of Abraham and of Jesus Christ remains alive, makes hope possible, encourages new desire and arouses men to anticipated attainments of future possibility.

When all is said and done the increase of this love of God and neighbor remains the purpose and the hope of our preaching of the gospel, of all our church organization and activity, of all our ministry, of all our efforts to train men for the ministry, of Christianity itself.

CONFUSING PROXIMATE WITH ULTIMATE GOALS

. . . Not long ago religion was often credited with the power and grace that belong only to the God of faith; religion, it was said, inspired, healed and saved.[4] Now that subjectivism is often replaced by another which puts the Church in the place of religion but confuses its work with that of its Lord and

---

4. The first two paragraphs and a portion of the third have been omitted. They return to the subject matter of theological education, now placed in the context of the Church and the goal of the increase of love of God and of neighbor. [Ed.]

equates devotion to it with loyalty to the kingdom of God. The resulting confusion is similar to the one that appears in political life when a particular democratic society is made the object of a devotion that genuine democracy extends only to humanity, created free and endowed with natural rights prior to any recognition of these facts. In the case of Communism it has become plain what internal contradictions and perversions ensue when the promotion of the party is substituted for the pursuit of the party's cause. That substitution has led to all manner of corruption. Christianity and the Church have not been slow to criticize Judaism because in it the idea of a people chosen for service was often converted into the idea of a people chosen for privilege while the victory of the cause which the people was chosen to promote was frequently equated with the victory of the people. It is always easy to discern the mote in the eye of another. The beam in our churchly or Christian eye is not so easily seen. Both in thinking of the context in which we work in the Church and of the goal we pursue, it seems easy to accept and propagate the idea that the last reality with which we are concerned is the Church itself, and that the summary commandment we obey is to love Christianity with heart, soul, mind and strength. This exaltation of Church or of Christianity leads us then to an effort not to reconcile men with God or to redirect their love and ours toward God and the neighbor but rather to convert them to Christianity. These purposes are not more identical than subject and object are identical. It is one thing to be reconciled to God and to conceive some love for the neighbor and hence to participate in the community of which Jesus Christ is the pioneer and founder; it is another thing to take for granted that if one is brought into membership with the historical society called the Church love of God and neighbor will automatically ensue.

It is evident that in dealing with this confusion we are attending to a subject that is important not only to theological education but to all the work of the churches. The confusion of a proximate, churchly, with the ultimate, divine, context and the attendant confusion of goals, lies at the heart of many dilemmas in which the Christian missionary enterprise is involved in its dealings with the adherents of other religions. It is close also to the problems of Protestantism in its encounters with the Roman Church. Having begun with protest against tendencies in the latter branch of Christianity to regard the Church as the representative of God it has often succumbed to the same tendency itself. In consequence it has found itself engaged in competition on the same ground its rival occupies and using weapons which its own principles deny to it. But if the confusion is serious in all other areas of Church action it is not the less serious in theological education. When it prevails such education necessarily becomes indoctrination in Christian principles rather than inquiry based on faith in God; or it is turned into training in methods for increasing the Church rather than for guiding men to love of God and neighbor. The confusion of the subject with the subject's object is more than an epistemological fallacy.

A similar confusion to which Protestantism is even more prone ensues when the Bible is so made the center of theological education that the book takes the place of the God who speaks, and love of the book replaces devotion to the One who makes himself known with its aid. The problem of the relation of Scriptures to revelation, of the Word of God spoken through the prophets and incarnate in Jesus Christ to the living Word, is one that has greatly concerned theology especially since the days of the Reformation. It is of particular importance in contemporary discussion. But it is not necessary to await the outcome of a long debate before one arrives at the conclusion that whatever else is true about these relations, the identification of the Scriptures with God is an error, a denial of the content of the Scriptures themselves. To give final devotion to the book is to deny the final claim of God; to look for the mighty deeds of God only in the records of the past is to deny that he is the living God; to love the book as the source of strength and of salvation is to practice an idolatry that can bring only confusion into life. Without the Bible, as without the Church, Christians do not exist and cannot carry on their work; but it is one thing to recognize the indispensability of these means, another thing to make means into ends. There is much theological education that suffers from inadequate attention to the Biblical history of divine words and deeds; there is more that suffers from so close a concentration on these that the One to whom Scriptures bear witness is overshadowed by the witness. The lines between theological education and Bible study are hard to draw. Genuine Bible study is theological and genuine theology cannot succeed without Bible study. But there is a Biblicism that is not theological because it does not make God so much as Scriptures the object of its interest, and which depends for law and grace not on Father, Son and Holy Spirit but on Bible. This kind of Biblicism involves theological education as well as the churches in inner contradictions.

The most prevalent, the most deceptive and perhaps ultimately the most dangerous inconsistency to which churches and schools are subject in our time (perhaps in all the Christian centuries) arises from the substitution of Christology for theology, of the love of Jesus Christ for the love of God and of life in the community of Jesus Christ for life in the divine commonwealth. Once more we touch upon a problem with which theology in our time is deeply concerned, and which makes evident how much the reconstruction of theological education depends on the reconstruction of theology. Yet as in the case of Biblicism it is hardly necessary to await the outcome of many inquiries before concluding that substantial error involving many further confusions is present when the proposition that Jesus Christ is God is converted into the proposition that God is Jesus Christ. If the long story of the Trinitarian debate in Christendom is to be re-enacted in our present time its outcome may result in somewhat different formulations from those of the past, but scarcely in a substantive change of the affirmation that God is One and that however the doctrine of the *Personae* is stated it must still be affirmed that the Father is not the Son and the Son is not the Father and the Spirit cannot be equated with either. Yet in many churchly pronouncements the faith of Christians is stated as if their one God were Jesus Christ; as if Christ's ministry of reconciliation to the Creator were of no importance; as if the Spirit proceeded only from the Son; as if the Christian Scriptures contained only the New Testament; as if the Old Testament were relevant only insofar as it contained prophecies pointing to Jesus Christ; as if Jesus Christ alone were man's only hope. When this is done the faith of Christians is converted into a Christian religion for which Jesus Christ in isolation is the one object of devotion and in which his own testimony, his very character, his Sonship, his relation to the One with whom he is united, are denied.

This kind of Christian religion has many forms. It is present in popular forms that are similar to Eastern Bhakti and Amida Buddha faiths. It is present in a liberal cult of Jesus and of "the Jesus way of life"; present also in mystical forms as the cultivation of personal companionship with the divine Christ. Historically and theologically we are dealing here with devout yet aberrant forms of faith that are unable to illuminate the more profound problems of human existence, suffering, guilt and destiny or to answer questions about human history in its wholeness. They tend moreover to make of that faith a religion much like all other human religions instead of a relation to the Transcendent that goes beyond all our religions. This confusion of the proximate with the final introduces many internal conflicts into the work of the churches and of theological education. It leads directly to the effort to emphasize the uniqueness of the Christian religion, to define it as the "true" religion, to recommend it because of its originality, to exaggerate the differences between Christian and Jewish faith, to re-erect walls of division that Jesus Christ broke down, to exalt the followers of the one who humbled himself, to define the neighbor as fellow Christian. That the confusion has not led to greater spiritual disasters than have been encountered is doubtless due to the fact that Jesus Christ in his nature and witness is a constant corrective of the perversion of his worship.

Denominationalism not the denominations; ecclesiasticism not the churches; Biblicism not the Bible; Christism not Jesus Christ; these represent the chief present perversions and confusions in Church and theology. There are many other less deceptive, cruder substitutions of the proximate for the ultimate. But the ones described seem to set the great problems to faith and theology in our time. In them the need for a constant process of a radically monotheistic reformation comes to appearance.[5]

5. A final transitional paragraph has been omitted. [Ed.]

PART III

The Churches and the Whole Human Community

My primary concern today . . . is still that of the reformation of the church. I still believe that reformation is a permanent movement, that *metanoia* is the continuous demand made on us in historical life. The immediate reformation of the church that I pray for, look for, and want to work for in the time that may remain to me is its reformation not now by separation from the world but by a new entrance into it without conformity to it.

H. Richard Niebuhr, "Reformation: Continuing Imperative" (1960)

10

The Gift of the Catholic Vision [1948]

What is the gift which has been given to theology in our time and which it has to offer to the Church and perhaps to the world? We need to think now not of the gifts which as the theology of Christians it, with all the other enterprises and all other offices in the Church, seeks to accept and communicate—the gift of the Gospel, the gifts of faith, hope, and love. Nor do we attend to those special gifts which individuals have received in their various measure—gifts of action and of thought, of learning and insight, of critical and constructive ability—though theology seeks to understand the granting of these talents as it pursues its great theme of the grace of God. We need rather to think now of the gifts given to theology as theology, as a special enterprise in the Church. When we do this it may seem to us that of the many favors granted to it in our day one deserves our special gratitude and attention—*the gift of the Catholic vision*. This is not a talent in which we desire to or can take pride, as though it distinguished us from our immediate predecessors to their disadvantage and our advantage. It is not a privilege which we are allowed to display but a trust we are required to administer. Yet it is a gift; and surely a part, perhaps a large part, of our immediate task as theologians lies in our apprehension and communication of it.

I

It is genuine *gift*, for we have not as theologians or as members of the Church set ourselves the task of acquiring this vision or point of view. It has not been granted to us because we have merited it. Moreover, it has been given us by means of many agencies and processes which had no real prevision of the end they were serving. We have received it, first of all, as an inheritance from the labors of that great liberal scholarship of the past centuries which usually had no notion that this would be the result of its labors. As Biblical scholarship its express interest, at times, was the emancipation of Christians and of theology from the Scriptures. Yet the consequence of its labors has been a greater pre-occupation with the thought of Biblical writers, a greater immersion of men into Biblical times and ideas than have characterized any preceding age of the-ology. To be sure the very same period which brought theology into closer touch with the Bible was a time in which the mass of Christians were led fur-ther away from Biblical interest and understanding. Yet it remains true that theology as a result of these Scriptural studies has been challenged to an unusual awareness of the thought and, ultimately, of the faith of the men of the Bible, which means that it is no longer able to approach its subjects with-out doing so in the constant companionship of the prophets and apostles, of the early and the later people of the covenant.

Similarly, the liberal movement which on its systematic side was often highly modernistic, seeking to construct theology on the basis of present reli-gious experience, developed an historical scholarship which introduced and introduces theologians to the company of the Church Fathers, of medieval and Protestant leaders so that henceforth they cannot think at all save as those who lived in active interchange of thought with their fellow-workers of the past. Often the avowed aim of such historical scholarship was the emancipation of the present from the past. History of doctrine was believed to show how rel-ative to their own time and irrelevant to ours the ideas of earlier generations were. The same Harnack who believed that emancipation from the Old Tes-tament was not only the possibility but the duty of the Church in his day brought his *History of Dogma* to a close with the reflection that Luther repre-sented the end of the history of dogma, since now it had become evident again that the Gospel was a matter of inner life and inner attitude rather than of rea-sons and beliefs. Yet he contributed what he did not intend to contribute—a sense of our participation in the life and thought of the whole Church. McGif-fert, to whom all things had become new, nevertheless made the past live again in his lectures and his books. Troeltsch, whose historical studies led to the rad-ical formulation of the problem of relativism, made us aware of the similarity of the problems which confront Christianity in all periods, whether Catholic or Protestant. One cannot study his *History of Christian Social Teachings* with-out becoming conscious of one's kinship to the men of centuries gone by and of the continuity both of social problems and of Christian responses to them. If, on the one hand, this historical scholarship of liberalism has left to us the difficult problems of historical relativism, it has made us contemporaneous, on the other hand, with the relative ages that have gone by and at the same time has brought into our present, as our counsellors and fellow-inquirers, the Churchmen of other ages. It will not do to say that the liberal historians thought to do evil but God thought to do good; they did indeed seek to do good, but the good they accomplished in requiring and enabling us to think *with* the whole Catholic Church and *in* the whole Catholic Church was a different good from the one they purposed.

If liberalism and modernism were the most obvious movements through which the gift of the Catholic vision has been given to contemporary theology, other evident agencies have also contributed to the same result. The theologies of divided Churches have been brought into unity by their common conflict with and adjustment to ecumenical movements outside the Church. What shall we say, for instance, of the role of a universal science with which theology has lived in uneasy relations of combat and alliance and armistice for the past three hundred years? In our efforts to deal with the questions science put to theology we have been forced to fall back on our common Christian faith, to discover and realize its distinctiveness, to explain at least to ourselves its metaphysical implications. The problems raised here cut across the issues we raised and which divided us within the Christian community. In the course of our reflections and inquiries in this sphere we were inevitably made aware of a companionship in the Church which the confessional divisions between various groups of Protestant Churches and even between Protestant and Roman Churches could not destroy. Of greater importance have been the challenges of our civilization, in its glory and its shame, and the raising anew of the problems of the Church's relation to the world. The Social Gospel was a movement in the whole Church, in which the various groups participated in their particular fashion. The result was not simply interdenominationalism and co-operation but the acceptance of a point of view which was super-denominational or undenominational. Again, there has been the emergence of communism as a genuinely ecumenical movement. The living and fruitful conflict with that new religion and new organization of life has had a certain external effect, of course, in persuading Christians to rally together. But its internal effects on the thought of the Church, and on theology in particular, are at least of equal importance, for the intellectual debate has led to new searchings of soul and mind on the Christian side as a result of which a new[,] yet old, sense of history, of the presence of a non-human determinism, of the mystery of human life as a whole, of the reality of the fall and of many another common insight of the universal Church have assumed fresh pertinence. Many other movements and experiences, of course, have been the occasions for the granting of the gift of the Catholic vision: the shrinking world, the mobility of the population, the re-emergence of the great tragic questions about human societies and empires, the renewal of the mystery of Israel. We cannot trace for ourselves, as a later time may be able to do, the ways in which our theology has been molded and guided. It may even be that other talents than the Catholic vision will seem of greater importance from the point of view of the future. Yet we are conscious, I think, of the fact that it is a genuine gift—given, not merited, real and not imagined.

II

If we try to define what this gift is we proceed most reasonably, perhaps, by beginning negatively, saying what the vision is not. It is evident, first of all, that the Catholic vision is *not the mystic vision*. The mystic vision is the sight or the immediate presence of the objects with which theology is concerned; moreover, it is a presence to the individual in his solitariness. It is a vision men have one by one and if it results in theology it can only issue in the sort of theology which undertakes to direct men to the measures they must take in order that they may have the private vision or which tries to describe how the miracle of vision takes place. When we see in companionship with others and communicate with each other about that which we see, and correct each others' understanding or interpretation of the seen, and supply one another with patterns by means of which to apprehend the self-presented object, we cannot speak of mystical vision. Though there is immediacy in all such sight it is not purely immediate but dependent on the presence of mediators and interpreters. We need not and ought not make it a matter of pride that our vision is not the mystical vision of men in their solitariness. We may even crave this gift for ourselves because others have had it. Yet the Catholic vision, the vision of men in a companionship of interpretation and communication with one another as well as with a common object, is something different.

The Catholic vision is evidently *not a national vision*. To be sure we are all members of nations and conditioned by national culture so that we interpret what we see and hear with the aid of patterns inherited from our particular national society. But it seems evident to us now that we have usually greatly overestimated the independence of a national culture and that, whatever may have been the situation in former times, we are not allowed even if we would to understand what we hear and see simply in the company of other Christian members of our nation. We recognize, I think, that there has never really been such a thing as an American theology whatever modifications theology may have experienced when expressed in the idiom of America. The Puritanism, Anglicanism, Lutheranism, and sectarianism with which we began our national life were not the products of thought and endeavor in America. The theologies which arose out of them, such as those of Edwards and Finney and

Bushnell, were not only related to the common roots of an ecumenical evangelical Christianity but were influenced by a worldwide movement of revival which was English as well as American, Continental as well as Anglo-Saxon, Roman Catholic as well as Protestant. As the Reformation was not only a Protestant but also a Roman Catholic event so the great revival of religion in the eighteenth century, in which our so-called American theology of the early period had its sources, was an ecumenical movement showing remarkable similarities in all its various phases and places of occurrence.

Or if we take that other high point in our theological development which we have sometimes called peculiarly American—the Social Gospel—we now understand that it was also a phase of a Catholic event. It had many spokesmen besides Gladden, Rauschenbusch and their American associates; Frederic Ozanam, Bishop Ketteler, Leo XIII, F. D. Maurice, Bishop Gore, the Blumhardts, Ragaz, and Kutter—these were spokesmen of a Catholic and of no provincial American movement. Again we may attend to that kind of activism which has sometimes been called peculiarly American by its friends and foes; then we remind ourselves that insofar as it is simple Pelagianism it flourished long before America was discovered. Had not Jerome regarded it as the typical product of porridge-sodden Britain while others thought to account for it, as well as for its Augustinian antagonist, by blaming the North African environment for the production of such vagaries? As we have been emancipated politically from the illusion of isolationism, understanding that we are not only now a part of the whole world but always were, so theologically we have come to see that there never was a distinctively American point of view from which the objects of theology could be peculiarly well seen or peculiarly well interpreted. Yet if, perchance, there ever was such an American vision, we know we do not have it now, whatever the incidental effects of our geographical and historical location. In politics and economics we doubtless cannot wholly avoid an American point of view and an American vision whether we regard them as gifts or limitations; in theology, as in physics, chemistry, and mathematics, there are no such things.

The Catholic vision, moreover, is *not a confessionalistic vision*. We are not confined any longer to the standpoint of a denomination nor to converse with companions who share the particular preconceptions of some division of the Church. This again has not been the result of our striving but has been given as a gift which often we have received only under compulsion. It has not been easy for most Protestants to accept Thomas Aquinas as one of their theologians; they have been convinced against their will that he, with all his faults, was also a servant of the truth in Christ and that he could direct their eyes toward what they had not previously known to be visible. It has been and remains difficult for many theologians to accept Martin Luther as one of their companions with whom they are bound to converse; it has been hard for some to welcome John Wesley and for others to receive John Calvin. But these giants have introduced themselves into the company of those with whom we converse and with whom we interpret, and there is now no way in which we can rid ourselves of their presence, their advice, and counsel. We sit in a Parliament or Congress where we must listen to the voices of a loyal opposition and cannot at will depart into rump meetings. We have found, moreover, that the Protestantism of Luther and Calvin implies much more Catholicism than we had imagined, that the theology of Wesley was far more Calvinistic than we thought, that the confessions of the Reformation presupposed the ecumenical creeds more positively than once seemed possible to us. We have found ourselves in our denominations and confessions debtors to one another, dependent on each other to such a degree that the confessionalist vision is no longer possible, however great our appreciation is of the value of the particular family to which we belong. We find ourselves working under a common constitution, which guarantees and limits our state rights, but we no longer live merely in the state. We cannot do so though we try.

Finally, we may say by way of negative definition that the Catholic vision of our theology is *not the cultural vision*, the vision from and in our particular civilization. In one sense that statement is, of course, too extreme to be true, for we are conditioned by our culture far more than we are by our nation. Our language and our thought-forms, our art and science, our economics and sense of history are too much a part of us for us to emancipate ourselves from our culture. It is also true that we are deeply concerned about our civilization, as Augustine was concerned for Rome, not because it is civilization but because it is an organization and a discipline of human lives on which persons in communities and communities of persons are dependent. But, on the other hand, we have seen that the Church which was resident in Jewish culture and then in Greco-Roman, and then in medieval, and now in modern civilization, is still one Church. As we have noted above, the very efforts of modernism to persuade us that we had no identity with the Church in Greco-Roman culture—efforts which unfortunately are echoed by some of the post-liberals—have served to convince us of the similarity of our interests and concerns and of the identity of our fundamental faith with those of the Christians who lived in that culture. Moreover, we have now come to regard with a certain resignation, if with a heavy heart, the possibility of the end of this modern period and to look with wonder not unmixed with apprehension at the possibilities of Christianity in the setting of Eastern culture or of a new Western civilization. Under these circumstances we have been compelled to attempt to view our civilization from the vantage point of a Church which is resident in many cultures, rather than to view the Church from the standpoint of civilization. Our vision

remains conditioned by the culture of which we are a part, yet it does not seem
to be limited by it, for our companions in communication and in vision are
members of other cultures, while all of them are citizens of the one *Civitas Dei*.

III

The negative description of what the Catholic vision is not has not only pre-
pared the way for a positive description but has in part included it. Hence we
may undertake to state rather briefly what it is. For one thing it is *vision*. It is
not simple converse among the thinkers of the Church about words and
thoughts which pass back and forth between them. Certainly theology like
philosophy can and often does suffer from this sterile sort of communication
which eventually—as ideas and words are abstracted from the entities to which
they refer—becomes logorrhea and logomachy. There can be a kind of
Catholic communication which is without vision. It speaks of ideas of atonement in Anselm and Bushnell, of theories of justification in Paul and Luther,
of thoughts about natural law in Thomas and Brunner, of conceptions of revelation in Barth and Calvin, of views of the sacraments in Augustine and
Zwingli, without ever raising its eyes to the realities about which these men
were and are thinking, theorizing, and speaking. Against such vacuous theol-
ogizing no time is proof nor is any discipline of theology guarded against it.
Biblical theology suffers from it no less than historical, philosophical theology
no less than systematic. The gift of Catholic vision is not the gift of Catholic
conversation simply; it is the gift to see and to hear, not first of all those who
look with us and hear with us, but to hear and see what is beyond them and us
together. It is the vision directed toward the revelation of God in Christ,
toward the Christ who is not first of all the spirit in the Church but the Lord
it encounters, toward the Word carved on tables of stones and nailed on a
wooden cross, not echoed within, toward the atonement that is independent
of our view of it, toward the kingdom and the law that rule and judge us from
a throne that is lifted high above us. In this sense, too, Catholic vision is not
mystic for it is directed toward the objective and the independent rather than
toward the subjective and internal. The theology of our predecessors and our
theology can both be characterized by reference to the double prepositions
each employs. The favorite preposition of liberal theology is *within*, of the
post-liberal *over against*. It was the gift of the earlier movement to understand that "the kingdom of God is within you"; of the contemporary one to
see that it is over against us. So with the word of God, which for the one "is
nigh thee, in thy mouth and in thy heart" and for the other "is living and active
and sharper than any two-edged sword, and piercing even to the dividing of

soul and spirit." The gift of Catholic vision is the gift of objective view. None will maintain that this gift cannot be and is not being abused, even as the gift of subjectivism has been abused. Yet it remains a gift of seeing that which is over against us.

Vision, however, is not independent of companionship. It is dependent on companionship for both interpretation and verification. We do not see save as we interpret what is over against us and we do not interpret save as we live in a community of interpreters. That community of interpreters for us has come to be the Catholic community, in time and space, as well as in inclusiveness of special functions and special views. I have said enough about the inclusiveness in time and space and confession of the community in which theology today carries on its work. Let me add only this that it has been granted us to work in a *living* tradition, free from slavish dependence on the views of others because with them we are directed toward that which is viewed, yet bound for our own sakes to their companionship in a community of interpretation as well as in the community of faith.

There is another catholicity, however, besides the temporal and spatial one; it is the companionship of those who are entrusted with special and various functions. Both a greatness and a weakness of the liberal theology lay in its specialization of functions. Biblical studies were Biblical studies and nothing else while systematic theology was often effectively insulated against historical and philosophical theology. These walls of partition are being broken down. Biblical studies are becoming theological, and systematic theology is becoming more Biblical; historical theology is aware that it is dealing with contemporary issues, and contemporary theology knows that it is carrying on an historical work, using, correcting and revivifying the past rather than leaving it behind. There are even indications that the philosophy and the theology of Christians may begin to work with greater knowledge and appreciation of what the other hand is doing. Doubtless the gift in this aspect has its dangers and the taking of the gift imposes great burdens upon us. Yet it is a gift and it is a great joy to know that we are not working alone but that theology is a common enterprise of many groups, each of them servant to the others. Theology has become and promises to become to an increasing degree a common enterprise not only as between the men of various times, countries, and confessions, but as between the inquirers in the several departments of the work.

Two other definitions of the gift of Catholic vision seem possible. It is vision from the standpoint of the Catholic *Church* and for us in the evangelical Churches it is *Protestant Catholic* vision. As Church vision it is the *outlook* and the insight of a theology that is part of the Church, which carries on its work for the Church, through the Church and in the Church. On the one hand it is the critical enterprise in the Church whereby its message, action, and organization are defined and corrected from within by reference to its internal reality and constitution. On the other hand it is confessional theology which seeks to set forth for the Church the corrected meaning of what the Church believes, understands, and sees. Again, it is apologetic theology which undertakes to set the Church's understanding into relation, negatively and positively, with those convictions about man and his ultimate environment which are associated with other faiths. It is polemic theology attacking the ideas and faiths by which men are led astray. But in every case it is Church theology. The gift of the Catholic vision is the gift of being allowed and required to stand in the Church and with the Church. Whether the gift of standing alone is a greater one may be subject to dispute. But, at all events, it is not the gift of our time nor our possibility and requirement.

Further, we may say that Catholic vision means for us in the evangelical part of the Church *Protestant Catholic* vision. It does not lead to Catholic Protestantism. There can be no Catholic Protestantism historically or logically. If it were a Catholic Protestantism historically it would exclude the companionship of non-Protestants not only in the contemporary world but in the past. It would banish not only Thomas but also Augustine from the company of interpreters. It would eliminate not only Ignatius of Loyola but also Bernard of Clairvaux. It would dismiss not only the Decrees of Trent from consideration but also the Nicene confession and the Chalcedonian formula. Historically also, as we are well aware today, Luther and Calvin no less than Hooker and Melanchthon need to be understood as members of the company of the Catholic Church. They conversed not only with the prophets and apostles but also with their later interpreters. To begin to speak with Luther is to begin to speak with Occam and with Biel, though as men who need to be corrected. Logically, Protestantism implies something that is protested against as Reformation implies something to be reformed. One cannot make a Catholic principle out of protest or an organizing principle out of reform. As Protestant Catholics we protest both against the absolutizing or deifying of the whole Catholic Church of which we are a part and against the claim of a part of that whole to exercise power over the whole. But it was a sad day for us when we surrendered the name Catholic to that part of the Church which failed in its catholicity, and so—as well as in other ways—failed in catholicity ourselves. As *Protestant* Catholic theology our theology will maintain the Catholic vision as embodying a continuous protest against the substitution of any finite reality including the Church for the sovereign of the Church—a substitution of which not only Romanism has been guilty. And as Protestants we will protest in the Church against seizure of power in the Church by any part. But the gift of the Catholic vision does not allow us to exclude from our companionship those against whom we protest for they are parts of the Catholic Church. It is the gift and duty of Protestant Catholicism to be more Catholic than Romanism is, to be in short the movement of Catholic reformation. For reformation there must be as long as there is Catholic Christianity.

IV

As we regard this gift of the Catholic vision granted to theology in our times our first reaction may be one of doubt and fear; though not unaccompanied by joy, yet it will be fundamentally hesitant. The gift, we may believe, is truly presented to us in our time, but how can we ever possess it? How shall we in our freedom master what is freely given? How shall we learn to employ the talent entrusted? Moreover, in view of the urgent needs of our time we may question whether this gift is the one we need in order that we may give to our world what it needs.

Second thought, however, tends to dispel some of these doubts. We cannot possess what has been given unless we use so much of it as we have been able to grasp. We cannot tell what needs it will meet until we give it to those in need. It may be after all that the greatest need of our world is not the need of a catholic state but that of a Catholic Church. And it may be that our use of the gift will bring forth good which we do not intend, just as the liberals' use of their gifts issued in values different from those they desired. We accept the warning of the parable of the talents and instead of burying this talent attempt to employ it as a working capital. So we ask what the uses are to which we can put the Catholic vision. How shall we employ it?

We note the double task we have as theologians. We are instructors and we are students. As instructors our question is how we may use Catholic vision in our teaching. Perhaps the answer is that if we have it we will not be able to refrain from communicating it, whatever else we try to communicate. Yet it does seem that more is required than simply to let the light shine. At least the bushel that is over the light needs to be removed. That bushel, it seems to me, is our present method of theological education, with its separation of the various specialists into isolated compartments, with its reliance on contemporary texts, and with its geographical and confessional segregation of students. In all respects there is a ferment at work in our schools and in our instruction. We are beginning to explore the possibilities of common work as between Biblical and systematic theology, between Church history and social ethics. Yet everything here remains experimental; we shall continue to fumble until we realize the problem more clearly and make more effective use of the challenge and opportunity of this particular day. Then we shall become colleagues instead of associated instructors. We are beginning to make larger use of the great classical treatises of the Catholic Church, though for the most part our instruction continues to employ too many second-hand interpretations. Perhaps some seminary will endeavor to do in theology what St. John's College has tried in the sphere of liberal arts. We may note a beginning in the development of ecumenical schools of theology if, indeed, the beginning was not made long ago. This project needs, however, to become the conscious interest of the Church and of theologians in many schools, not only in the interdenominational but also in the denominational centers; for the Catholic vision, I believe, does not preclude but rather demands the employment of the special gifts entrusted to Calvinists, Lutherans, Anglicans, Methodists, etc., though it does mean their communication to those who are not members of the particular families concerned.

In the field of study the Catholic vision provides us with a starting point for new approaches to the perennial theological questions and to those old problems which have a novel importance in our day. There is the problem of religious knowledge, of reason and faith, of revelation and discovery, of intuition and discursive knowledge, of practical and theoretical reason. In a Catholic Church the various interests and emphases with respect to this problem are represented by contending schools none of which, in their actions and reactions, loses its sense of being engaged with all the others in one great inquiry, and all of which strive for that larger knowledge which is not exclusive but inclusive. The synthesis of Thomas Aquinas is not available to us now; and every synthesis we shall manage to formulate in the future will doubtless be the occasion for a new antithesis. But Catholicism is fruitful debate in which each party is led beyond itself in the common search for understanding.

There is the problem of God. In our period of individualism and sectarianism we have been unitarians—theo-centrists, Christo-centrists, spirito-centrists. We have developed the doctrine of God the creator, the doctrine of God in Christ, the doctrine of the immanent God more or less independently of each other. The Catholic vision leads us to an understanding of the limitations of our peculiar doctrines of God first of all, and then to a recognition of the dependence of our understanding on that of others. It makes us share the objective vision of many comrades and brings to view some wonders of the divine reality which in our partiality we had not contemplated. It is my own conviction that Catholic vision leads to Trinitarian doctrine, not because Trinitarian thought is traditional, but because the tradition helps us to understand modes of being, action, and relation in the reality, which is as present to us as to the men of Nicea. Yet the Trinitarianism of our Catholic vision will doubtless be somewhat different from the Trinitarianism of the Catholic view of the fourth century, however continuous the doctrines may be.

The Catholic point of view brings us into sight of the atonement in a different manner than was available to us in the isolation of private religious experience or from a point of view that made the God-consciousness of the redeemer its object. We are led to inquire into the objectivity of an event and a process that is not simply within us but over against us, which concerns us not only as persons but as a community, and concerns us not only as the community of the Church but as the community of mankind in its never-to-be-repeated history.

Finally, Catholic vision moves the Church into a new perspective. For now we see that the human response to divine action is not so much religion as Church. It is not the Christian religion with which we are concerned, as our predecessors were concerned with it, but the *ecclesia* which worships, to be sure, which has religious ideas and religious rites, but which is something more inclusive and more strange than a religious association. What is this body of Christ, this *Civitas Dei*, this new people? It stands in succession to and is akin to that other strange community of Israel which is not simply a religious society nor yet a political or a racial community. The church always tends to retreat into religion and to become the religious institution of a civilization but cannot remain content with that role. Its members forever transcend the boundaries of what men call religion; they form sects, societies within society yet apart from society; they enter restlessly into the political and economic life of the civilizations in which they dwell; they seek a Zion which cannot be located in any part of earth and yet are not content to find their beatitude one by one in a heavenly Paradise. It is a pilgrim community which makes strangely enduring settlements. It is an abnormal community which does not fit into this world and yet forever seeks to make itself at home in a world that is a Fatherland. It has a King and a land of its own, to which it appeals beyond all the rulers and laws of men, but the King is invisible and the law is impractical; and yet, all other kings are powerless before him and all the laws save his impractical. The mystery of the Church and the wonder of the Church present themselves to the Catholic view for new inquiry, new interpretation, and then for new reformation and new direction.

So our work in theology takes its place alongside those other enterprises of the Church to which the political events of our time and the great ecumenical councils call attention. In part we serve them, in part we express in thought what they express in other sorts of action. For Catholicism is as much an affair of the mind as it is of the organization of the Church. We cannot live in the Catholic Church save as the Catholic Church is also in us, in our minds and spirit; it cannot be in us, however, save as we also live in it. Among the joys which the Catholic vision has brought there is this joy—that we know our theology to be one work in a many-sided enterprise in which we serve and are being served. And beside that joy there is another one—that as theologians we are also members of one another, dependent on each other even when we differ, serving each other even when we are divided. The gift of the Catholic vision brings to our awareness what has always been true—that we believe in, that we count upon, the Holy Catholic Church in which we are and which is among us.

11

The Churches and the Body of Christ
[1953]

The relation of the community of Christ to religious societies, institutions and organizations is one of the constant problems of Christians. It has a peculiar poignancy in our time when the desire for community is so strong among men. This desire manifests itself in the first place as a searching and hungering for intimate, warm and reliable companionship. Everywhere men are seeking what they call security, but which is often identifiable as the sense of belonging, of being wholly accepted, supported and valued by a fellowship, which, moreover, directs them to significant work.

Many reasons may be given for the appearance in our time of this search for community. Among them one may name the depersonalization that is characteristic of a technological and industrial civilization; the growth of the cities and the breakdown of large family units; the loss of intimate relation with the soil and the life of nature; the high mobility and rootlessness of a population that changes residence not only in consequence of wars and oppressions but of the attraction of better wages and living conditions; the substitution of external relations for internal ones. In the language of sociology, we tend to live today in societies rather than in communities. Societies are combinations of individuals which do not profoundly modify the internal character and sense of selfhood that individuals possess; they are contract associations which men form and join for the sake of achieving limited common ends and which they can leave or dissolve without leaving a part of themselves behind. Communities, on the other hand, are far more intimate in their interactions. Commu-

The William Penn Lecture delivered at Race Street Meeting House, Philadelphia, Pennsylvania, on November 8, 1953. As published by The Young Friends Movement of the Philadelphia Yearly Meetings.

nities exist in the individual as individuals exist in them. A community is warm and personal—a union of whole lives rather than of the fractional interests of individuals. A business partnership is an example of society; the family is the primary instance of community. It is community, not society that men are seeking in our time; of society they have their fill; but for community they hunger and thirst.

A second widely recognized aspect of this modern search is the desire for *universal* community. Men seek the security of close friendship, the intimacy of family life; but they also want inclusiveness and breadth in their common life. Their desire for community is for world community, for universal friendship. The realization of the unity of all the tribes and nations of mankind, of all the groups with their various histories and hopes, arises before the eyes of our generation as a possibility and as a goal zealously to be sought. Conversely, we experience the division of men as tragedy and as threat. Strangely enough the threat to our existence does not arise from our division only but from division mated with the demand for unity. If we were content to be divided into many groups, co-existing with each other without interpenetration there would be no threat. But we must have one community, we believe. In part, doubtless, the strife of ideologies and nations that is characteristic of our day is just another chapter in the story of imperialism. But something else is present besides the tendency of every human group to universalize itself. The great mass movements of the past century and a half derive much of their meaning and appeal from their effort to meet the human demand for universal community.

There is a third aspect to this searching for community. We are experiencing our isolation and our division not only as a separation of man from man, human group from human group, but as an alienation of man from his world. Man feels himself alone in an empty or inimical world over which chance or blind will presides. He has no sense of being at home under the sky and upon the good earth; the earth is not his mother and there is no father in the heavens. Orphaned, anxious and alone he finds himself with his fellows wandering through time on paths that lead to no home. Yet he is filled with a great nostalgia and envies with a certain wistfulness those generations that believed themselves to be living in a Father's house or, at least, to be engaged in a pilgrimage that led daily nearer to the quiet hearth at the center of the world.

Whether we are most aware in this quest for community of the longing for familiar security or of the hope for universal peace or of the desire for a revelation of love at the heart of things, yet we know that all these things are tied together and that there is a religious element in all our seeking. The quest for community is not only always religious, it is expressed in the specifically religious movements of our time. One of these movements is the movement toward Christian faith on the part of thousands of men in our world who have no traditional or acknowledged relation to any of the churches or other groups called Christian or by some other religious name. Feeling themselves isolated and spiritually starved in our secular civilization they seek a community that has a wide view of this mysterious scene of human existence, a sense of at-homeness in it despite its mystery, a feeling for and an understanding of its tragedy, a sense also of reconciliation to life and to all the members of the community of life. The church rises before their view as the community they seek. Yet such men often cannot reconcile themselves to any of the established Christian organizations. These seem to them to be lacking either the intimacy or the breadth of the community towards which they aspire. So they continue to look upon them from a distance with a strange mixture of yearning and of contempt.

The problem of the church-community is no less keenly felt by many, perhaps by most, of those who are regarded as faithful members of the established and recognized Christian societies or as devout participants in the habitual, institutional practices of the Christian religion. They may regard the expressions of belief characteristic of these societies with much scepticism; or they may bewail the lack of genuine love among the members of the group. Whatever their reasons and whatever the rationalizations of their true, yet often unknown, reasons, they have not found in the Christian societies to which they belong the community they seek. They are often lovers of the church, and yet do not love the church to which they belong, which they see and hear. This brittle relation of man to the Christian societies seems widespread; it is to be encountered in Roman Catholicism and in Protestantism; in the minority sects as well as in the mass churches. The line between the unchurched lovers of the church and the churchly seekers after a church beyond the churches is often difficult to define.

The quest for the church as a community broad, intimate and deep is expressed today also in the ecumenical movement. This movement, to be sure, has many sources as well as many expressions. It is not easily defined as a single movement though the term is most usually associated with the effort to organize councils and federations of Christian societies that will associate in common action groups otherwise divided by national and denominational barriers. This unity of organization is sought in part in order that the various Christian groups may present a more effective resistance or challenge to secularizing and anti-religious powers. But organization is also the sign and instrument of a sense of oneness between men of various countries and historical religious divisions who have hitherto lacked visible and effective means of communication and of participation in each others' thoughts, hopes, purposes and faith. The organizational phase of the movement is by no means necessarily its most important part. There is an ecumenical movement in our schools and in our culture as a whole. In our various Christian societies we are studying the thoughts of the intellectual leaders of other groups as we have not done since the days of the Reformation. Protestants read Augustine and Thomas Aquinas; Roman Catholics study Luther and Barth; some Methodists immerse themselves in the thoughts of Luther; Dissenters pay new homage to Anglicans. In the sphere of action we make use of each others' special gifts and organizations. When the Church of the Brethren undertakes to send heifers, sheep, seeds and poultry to devastated regions, it acts for and with the support of Christians who had previously scarcely known of its existence. The Service Committee of the Society of Friends becomes the agency of a far wider fellowship than that of the Society itself. In all of this we express our desire for a church beyond the churches, for a community of Christ, distinct from but not unrelated to the societies of national and denominational churches, associations and sects.

II

Urgent as these various movements toward the realization of a Christian community now are, it is erroneous to think of them as peculiarly modern. We say today that we seek such a community because industrial civilization has replaced our family sense of belonging together in one bundle of life by the external ties of contract, or substituted for the indissoluble covenant relationship in which we committed ourselves to each other completely the looser, ever dissolving relationships of common interests. But in other eras men also sought a church beyond the churches though they gave different reasons for their dissatisfaction with the societies with which they were allied. When the Society of Friends was founded in the 17th century its authors protested against the established church and the sects of that time with the use of other phrases than those we now employ, yet they also were alienated from the visible institutions and organizations; they also sought a community in which they might realize their hopes of intense fellowship with one another, with God and Christ in the Spirit. The Reformation was a search for the church beyond the churches. Though its central concern was with the authority of the Scriptures and with the experience of justification by faith through the personal apprehension of the Gospel yet it also aspired after a Christian "Gemeinde" in Luther's term, a Christian common life which the religious institution and the monastic societies of the day did not provide. The search after the church beyond the churches, after a community of Christ beyond all the Christian societies, is noticeably present in all the reform movements within Christendom since the beginning of the faith. It is present in the Franciscan movement, in the many reforms of the monastic life, in Augustinian aspiration after the City of God, in Paul's controversy with the Judaizers and in the efforts of the Hellenists in Jerusalem to provide for better care of their widows and orphans. The story of the old people of God, Israel, is no less a story of hunger and search after a Zion different from all the old and new Jerusalems of history.

Not only in the great movements of history but in all the personal stories of individuals in societies this drama of alienation from the societies of Christ or of God and of quest after a "city that has foundations" has been re-enacted. Of how many individuals must it not be said that they have been in and out of the church over and over again during their life-times? They have read themselves out and read themselves back in without giving any public notice of the fact. And these alienations and reunions of theirs have been guided to no small extent one may believe by their desire for genuine community in Christ, for communion with other men which would at the same time be reconciliation and friendship with the author and determiner of their existence. The quest for the church beyond the churches, for a society of friends and a brotherhood beyond all existing societies and fraternities has been an enduring quest of Christians throughout all their generations.

It seems to be more than a Christian movement—this aspiration after the City of God. When the Stoic called the world his fatherland and affirmed "Nothing is foreign to me that is not foreign to thee, O Zeus"; when the Chinese asserted that all men are brothers, they were giving utterance to a recognizably similar hope and desire. It is through Jesus Christ that the meaning of man's aspirations, the true direction of his spirit, has been brought most clearly to consciousness. It is through him that the reconciliation of man with man is most clearly realized to be dependent on his reconciliation with God; it is through him, also, that the road of repentance and faith has been opened. He begins, not by his teaching so much as by his appearance and his destiny, a new era in the story of man's hope for and quest for community. Yet the gospel of Christ is a gospel for the world precisely because it is addressed to all those who hunger and thirst after this goodness. The community of Christ which is the object of the Christian's hope is something more than the community of those who say "Lord, Lord" to him. It is the community of brothers through the mediation of the Son of God; it is community in the Spirit that proceeds from the Father and the Son, and therefore is a community that transcends all historical Christian societies.

III

The dissatisfaction that we feel with all our religious societies, our churches, sects, and institutions; the aspiration in men after a community that transcends all these can easily be idealized in undue fashion. When we think of these things we may be led astray into a self-pitying and self-congratulatory romanticism. We are tempted in Rousseauistic spirit to place the blame for all human failure to achieve ultimate community on the established institutions and perhaps on men who are thought to be using these institutions for narrow, personal or class ends. And with this analysis of the situation we often combine a hortatory idealism, persuading men to try and try again to achieve an ideal that through all the ages of the past they have been unable to realize. This way of dealing with the problem of the relationship of the community of Christ to the Christian societies is highly dubious.

Such idealism, attending to the aspirations of men after fraternity, like those after liberty and equality, hardly recognizes the fact that much of the dissatisfaction with the institutions and societies arises not out of the conflict of the expansive movements of the human spirit with the narrowness of institutions but out of the warfare of the private interests of the individual with the more universal concerns of the social bodies. Conflict arises not only because churches are nationalistic, historically relative and class-related, because they are under the dominance of official clergy and of narrowly defined creeds while individuals seek for a church beyond the churches. It arises also because each individual tends to desire a community centered around himself and his own particular needs, not necessarily in a selfish but nevertheless in a particularistic sense, while the churches and societies represent a wider circle of interests and convictions. Just as the ethics of institutions are in many respects more stable and more inclusive than the ethics of individuals, so also the principles of community maintained by the historical societies are frequently more tenable, less subject to emotional prejudice and partiality of insight than those of their dissatisfied members.

The individualistically or historically inspired movements of reform in which the search for a church beyond the churches has expressed itself offer us many examples of the advantage that the established societies have over the dissenters. One group of examples is offered by the aspiration after One, Holy and Catholic church. By and large the great Christian societies have sought, though in an evidently confused, imperfect and sinful manner, to hold fast to all three principles. The community they seek to represent, must have all three of these characteristics of unity, integrity, and universality. How difficult it is to maintain all three, the story of the protests shows. Dissatisfaction with the churches has expressed itself in the demand for unity at the expense of holiness and universality. The churches, many dissenters have said, lack that love, that warmth of personal concern of member for member that must characterize true community. If they were but more loving we could love them, but as it is we must seek a church beyond the churches, some intimate brotherhood, some cell, in which each of us feels himself surrounded and maintained by the devoted concern of his brothers. But that demand has often been associated with neglect of the principle of universality, so that now our Christian world is full of little family groups, "Familists" that claim to be the church in their achievement of unity, but which in their exclusiveness have rejected the principle of universality. More frequently the dissenters have taken issue with the churches' lack of holiness. In all ages they have called attention to the great difference between the practices and the professions of Christians in their societies. Ignoring the fact that this is every man's problem, that conflict between principles and desires is rarely if ever resolved in favor of principle all the time by any individual, the seekers after a holy community beyond the unholy churches have tended to incarnate their ideal community by means of Puritan, Holiness movements that resulted in the exclusion from their new "ideal" churches of the more conspicuous sinners among men. Yet again the universalists among the seekers for a church beyond the churches have been moved to found societies in which the particular principles of Christian holiness and of the love of Christ have been dissolved in vague tolerationism and humanitarianism. It is a melancholy fact that the division of the churches which we bewail in our search for the community of Christ has resulted to a very large extent from efforts to found the one true community that should take the place of existing, defective Christian societies. In the name of unity or holiness or of universality each particular organization has set itself up as representing better than all others the true community. In the name of unity, we disunite; in the name of holiness we reject wholeness and deny reverence to what God has made clean; in the name of universality we have become and continue to become particularists. It is easy to call attention to this fault; it is difficult if not impossible to eradicate it. We always see the mote in the institutional eye and fail to see the plank in the personal eye: we find our own ideas so reasonable, our own language so intelligible, that we cannot but try to make ourselves with our ideas the centers of the universe.

Another set of examples may be taken from the quest after human community with God. We cannot be at one with one another unless we are at one with the common cause, the common source, the common and overarching reality on which we all depend. We seek community with the One beyond the many as we seek our oneness with each other in church and world. Now the great institutions of Christendom have directed us to a communion with the Father and the Son and the Holy Spirit, One God, world without end. Dissent has often found this statement and the practices connected with it coldly intellectual and sterilely formal. No doubt they often are so. But the dissent itself has tended to substitute for communion with this One, known in nature and in history and in inner experience together, the communion with the one known only in nature, or the one known only in history, or with the one known only in inner experience. Naturalism and Deism, Christomonism and Jesus worship, spiritualism and mysticism have each seen themselves as alone representing true communion with God. So quest for a church beyond the churches has resulted in the development of practices of communion with God that have been inaccessible to other large groups of men. Once more the consequence has been the multiplication of new societies, new cults and rites, good doubtless in themselves or good for some but not means of grace to many others.

The kind of idealism which thinks so highly and so onesidedly of the inspirations of the individual and of dissenters in their groups, has tended to think badly of institutions and of established societies in general. Now the sobriety which comes from self-knowledge and the knowledge of history must qualify all such judgments. It does not lead us to idealize the existing societies, as though they were indeed incarnations of the community of Christ; on the contrary it also knows the pretentiousness and falsity of such claims. But at the same time it clearly sees that individuals do not excel the societies but that the same infections of pride, self-sufficiency, partiality, and all the attendant host of evils, are present in them quite as much as in societies. On the other hand this sober view recognizes values in the societies that no individuals in themselves, no matter how saintly, can possess.

IV

The situation in which we find ourselves in modern Christendom seems, then, to be something like this. We are deeply aware of our need for one, holy, universal community, in which we shall have fellowship with each other in our communion with God and in which our faith in God will appear in our loyalty to one another. We are highly aware of the artificiality of our divisions from each other in denominations, national churches and all the other societies of Christendom. We recognize also that all our efforts to achieve unity by means of new organizations, of Christian "defense communities," of federations and councils do not satisfy our need for life in a community of spirit. Yet we are aware at the same time of the healthful and necessary part the denominations, federations and all the other societal organizations of Christendom play in rescuing us from our individual isolations, in checking our efforts to make ourselves or our parties the centers of community, in mediating the great tradition of the community of men in Christ with God. We see that the societies stand in an ambivalent relationship to the community. On the one hand they are its deniers, on the other hand its representatives.

What can we do in this situation? What form shall our quest of the church beyond the churches take? Doubtless it will continue to issue in endeavors to achieve unions and federations of the denominations and other societies, yet we are well aware that all such efforts can only lead to new organizations in which the old ambivalent pattern of denial and affirmation of the One, Holy Catholic church will be expressed. Doubtless, also, the quest for the church beyond the churches will continue to take the form of an eschatological hope; we shall endure our divisions, and our dissatisfactions and disillusionments with the societies while we await the emergence of true community in an event that is not wholly continuous with present historical development. We shall say, "The realization of the one church, the community of the spirit, is one of those things that is impossible for men, but with God all things are possible." So in patience we shall wait for the coming of the great church and for the coming into our own lives of the unity of faith and the bond of peace.

Yet we can do something more than to wait in patience and to make our ever frustrated efforts to organize new societies more inclusive, or more unified, or more holy than those we see around us and to which we belong. We can realize the actuality of the church beyond the churches, of the community of Christ that is more than the sum of all the societies and that is something different in kind from these societies. In the realization of the actuality of that community we can so use our membership in the Christian societies and can so qualify the activities of these societies that they shall increasingly become servants of the community and members of it.

The community of Christ is more actual, more present, less merely future, more powerful in our lives than we usually realize. When we call it a spiritual reality we are likely to be misunderstood as meaning that it is not real but that it exists only in the minds of men. But the communities that exist in the minds, in the personalities and in the interpersonal relations of men, are often more real and powerful than the visible societies. The community of a nation, the network of interpersonal relations, of common loyalties, of memories and hopes, is a spiritual reality that is distinctly different from though related to, the social structure of states, governments, laws, political parties, etc. These are only instruments of the national spiritual community. To a much greater extent there is a community of Christ which is a common spiritual life, a common life of persons who are united to each other, to past and future by internal ties. There is a spiritual unity between Protestant and Roman Catholic Christians that can never be adequately defined in any formula of words stating a common creed, or can ever be adequately realized in action through the organization of inter-confessional societies for the achievement of common goals. We can only point to the reality of that community by referring to the common picture of the world and of history, of the common reliance on the government of God, of the common memory of Christ and the common hope of salvation. As soon as we try to formulate the common idea precisely we come into conflict; as soon as we endeavor to form some new society that will include both Protestants and Catholics we find ourselves involved in a power struggle, or in contention about the authority of various human organizations. What is true of Protestants and Catholics is true of all the other divisions in Christendom. There is a community of Christ and in Christ that is actual and that exerts its power over the minds and wills and emotions of us all. The societies are its instruments and partial expressions but no more than that. It is prior to them in power as well as in value.

Insofar as we consciously recognize the reality of this community in which we live, we begin to qualify the actions and claims of our various societies and begin, perhaps, to make them better instruments of the community. We no longer speak of our societies as the church but as agencies or orders of the church. We no longer consider ourselves, as individuals, to be members of the church by virtue of our membership in the societies but only by virtue of our belonging to Christ; we know that our membership in that body of Christ requires a kind of multiple membership in the societies. So one and the same man may be, as a member of the body of Christ, an active participant in the work of many Christian societies, as when he is, let us say, a Methodist, a worker in the Student Christian Movement, a member of the wider fellowship of the Friends, of a city federation of churches, and an active participant in some Catholic-Protestant venture. To realize the actuality of the community is to realize the relative character of the claims any particular society of Christians can make upon us and the necessity of regarding ourselves as related to the community of Christ and not vice versa—related to Christ through our societies.

The most adequate parable of the situation in which we find ourselves is the New Testament parable of the body of Christ. "For just as the body is one and has many members, and all the members of the body, though many, are one body, so it is with Christ" [1 Cor. 12:12, RSV]. The parable is misapplied if societies that always have some other head beside Christ call themselves the body of Christ. Every Christian society has in fact some other head besides Christ, be it Paul, Cephas, Apollos, the pope, Luther, Fox, Wesley, or any one of the many other apostles and prophets, or be it the king, the nation, the culture or any one of the other many principles that we associate with Christ. The parable is also misapplied if all the societies together are regarded as the body of Christ without reference to the head who is not in any of the members or in the totality of the members but always distinct from them. But it is an excellent and indispensable parable if the primacy of Christ in God and God in Christ is kept in view, and if we proceed not from the many societies to the one head but from the one head to the many societies.

With the aid of this parable we can understand our Christian societies, our relations as individuals to them and to the head as well as their relations to each other. We see the community of Christ as an actual community in the world, infinitely more complex than any human body, yet something like it. It is like a body in that it is made up of many members intricately interacting in common service, often in tension with each other, serving one another not only by way of positive help but also by balancing and checking each other. The body of Christ today, the community of Christ in the world, is as "fearfully and wonderfully made" as any of us are individually in our complex psychosomatic structure. Its rule is beyond our control. We cannot construct or reconstruct it. It is there and we are in it. We are in it as individuals and as societies. We are in it as those who need in the infinite activity of the body to operate together in ever new ways; perhaps as those who are being directed by the head to form new organs. But the reality and unity of the body do not depend on our understanding of its structure and on our efforts to supply it with unity or power.

In this faith in the reality of the holy, catholic church, of the community of Christ we can rejoice in the development of the many societies that are parts of its structure, accept our own particular societies with gratitude and without feelings of inferiority or superiority to other societies, accept with gratitude also these other societies with which and sometimes against which we must work, and go about our business of building up the community through the special and limited services we can perform in this our time and place. The church beyond the churches exists now. We know it only in part, to be sure, and for the rest accept it by a faith that does not see, yet is loyal to the unseen.

12

Reconciliation in an Ecumenical Age
[1960]

The ecumenical movement is manifold. It has many aspects and many sources. Two of its forms call themselves to our attention particularly—the institutional and the communal. Of these two the first is the more conspicuous. The ecumenical Church rises into view, is highly visible, in the appearance of scores of new organizations. World synods meet at Jerusalem, Edinburgh, Oxford, Amsterdam, Evanston. World councils are formed; bureaus established; services of care for one another are inaugurated. Denominations unite and publish their new constitutions; federations, leagues and councils of Churches are formed. Great buildings are erected to house their offices; busy executives correlate the work of their many agencies; represent the concerns of Protestant Christians to government offices and officers; call the attention of the public to the moral issues in our common life; defend the Churches against the attacks of the deluded and the frightened. This institutional movement is ecumenical on the one hand in antithesis to the provincialism or continentalism which confines Church organizations to particular geographic areas. The new institutions are those of a planetary parish and are the agencies of a community that has no regional or national boundaries. On the other hand the ecumenical Church is the one that crosses denominational boundaries and comes to appearance in cities and regions, in academic communities, in states and nations, in new institutions that operate alongside the well-known organs of confessional Churches. This double set of institutions

Address delivered at the inauguration of Dr. James I. McCord as President of Princeton Theological Seminary, March 29, 1960. An introductory paragraph referring to the occasion has been omitted. [Ed. note: An additional sentence referring to the seminary context has been omitted in this version. The address was published originally as "The Seminary in the Ecumenical Age."]

is the *visible* ecumenical Church—not, to be sure, in the old meaning of the term "visible Church" as the Church in which good and evil were still mixed together—though there are evidently those who want to apply this meaning primarily to the visible ecumenical *ecclesia*.

I

With the coming of this Church in our time the seminaries as such have not had much to do. Seminaries as such have not been its midwives or godparents. Presidents and deans and professors, to be sure, have as devoted and imaginative churchmen contributed not a little to the development of these visible institutions. But they have not made this contribution in following their special calling as Christian scholars and teachers. It has been in answer to other calls that they have served their Lord in this fashion. The long roster of Christian academics that can be collected from the list of founders and directors of ecumenical institutions simply serves to show how mythical is the popular picture of the scholar—the theological professor in particular—which portrays him as the absent-minded pursuer of ideal butterflies, oblivious to his solid, rock-strewn, practical social environment. The schools themselves also, as institutions with more than one calling in the Church of Christ, have labored at the building of the visible *ecclesia*. They have housed it; they have supplied it with workers; in their studios blueprints and designs have been drawn for this or that part of the cathedral which is being fashioned slowly in the course of generations and centuries, with many changes of plan and of material, but stubbornly and surely to the glory of God.

Yet it is less to the building of the visible than of the *invisible* ecumenical Church that the seminaries have given their labor. The *invisible* universal Church is, of course, first of all the Church in which we *believe*, this Church no man builds save as he is an instrument in the hands of its only real builder, Jesus Christ, the head of the Church, the one who works in present as in past in manifold ways beyond the possibility of description by means of our unimaginative, stereotyped formulae about his kingship, his prophecy and his priesthood. This invisible *ecclesia*, the company of those whom Christ saves, reconciles, intercedes for; this holy catholic Church that includes sheep from folds we have not dreamed of; this community, including angels and archangels and all the company of heaven, all who are elected by him to serve his cause, and to follow the leadership of the Son to the glory of God the Father: this Church does not belong to our time more than to any age gone by or coming. It is the company, the community, the cause in which men have trusted and to which they have sworn their oaths of allegiance since the day of Abraham if not since history began, as the history of social men who saw—beyond the limits of their tribes and nations, beyond the limits of their generations and their times—in dim vision, the reality of a universal and eternal society, the commonwealth of God.

It is not to this invisible Church of our faith that we refer when we speak of the invisible ecumenical movement, though it is certain that the latter exists only in dependence on the former. The invisible Church of the ecumenical age cannot be seen because it is present only to the *minds* of men, not because like the invisible Church of all the ages it is present in its fullness only to the mind of God. The invisible ecumenical movement is spiritual, but we cannot readily identify the spirit in us which testifies to it with that universal Holy Spirit which lives and moves in the universal and eternal Church of faith. The invisible ecumenical life is the movement toward a common Christian mind in our time, a movement that is both the precondition and the result of the development of ecumenical institutions, though it is more their presupposition than their consequence. For to a large extent we need to think of the present situation more as one in which an actual community of thinking, feeling, hoping persons in their many associations is seeking institutions in which to express itself, than as a time in which institutions seek to create inward, personal community. Before our nation, to use a parable, could fashion its political institutions it needed to become a community with a common mind and hope. Before colonial institutions could be supplemented by national [ones], the separate common minds of Virginians, Pennsylvanians and Vermonters needed to be transcended and included in the growth of a new common mind. That development of a common American mind, invisible for the most part, is an analogy to the invisible ecumenical movement of our age.

To it the seminaries have made the greatest contribution and unless they continue to foster it, the increase of the visible, institutional universal Church will at least be imperiled, if not become impossible. Of great importance to the development of a common mind in Protestant Christianity—if indeed not in all Christendom—has been the discovery or the uncovering of a common Bible. Nothing seems more evident than that we have had a common Bible from the beginning of Protestant Christianity at least. We have been able to understand each other and to argue with each other, to have significant rather than irrelevant differences with each other, because we have had the common Bible. Yet before there came into being the object-centered, Bible-centered scholarship that our theological schools have fostered now for a hundred and fifty years, we were unable to make the critical distinctions we now make between the objective Scriptures and the specific convictions we bring to their reading in our several confessional groups. We do not yet have a wholly common Bible; there remain among us those who find the self-evident key to the whole Scriptures in the opening verses of the Gospel of John; and those for whom all its sayings, reports, prophecies and gospels lead clearly toward or issue from Romans 1 to 5; and those for whom the indisputed focus lies in Matthew 5 to 7; or in the book of Revelation or even in some key to the Scriptures not itself in the canon. But we are now aware of these facts about ourselves. Our Biblical scholarship has enabled us to have more of a common Bible than we have ever had before in Christian history. And thus also to have more of a common mind as we read and interpret the Scriptures. To live in an ecumenical age without a common Bible is as impossible as to live in a truly international world without a common law. If we are somewhat further advanced in inter-Church affairs than the nations are in achieving international unity, then the gift and the achievement of a common Bible is in large part responsible. Doubtless it was not the intention of the schools to promote the growth of the ecumenical community by giving it a common Bible. The intention of our scholars and teachers in Biblical subjects has only been to forget themselves and to let the Bible speak for itself. But the consequence has been a movement toward a common mind. Biblical scholarship and teaching in most of our seminaries is now and has been for a long time ecumenical, both as interdenominational and international. This may be even truer of American schools than of those in Europe, at least so far as internationalism is concerned. But the movement of thought flows increasingly in both directions across the Atlantic and in time will do so across the Pacific, too.

II

An almost equally great contribution to the growth of the world Christian community has been made by our theological schools through their study and teaching of our history. In every present moment we are divided from each other more by the separating memories of our past encounters than by our immediate actions and reactions on each other. When the union of two churches in a New England village was attempted some years ago—because religious, doctrinal, sociological and economic conditions all pointed unmistakably toward that action as the fitting, right and good action—the plan was wrecked on a rock in the memory. One group recalled that 175 years ago it had been refused permission to erect its church on the village green and had been consigned to an ignoble side street. The memory of its members did not permit them to believe that they were now fully accepted; at least it did not permit them to look with disinterested eyes on the present situation. And who knows but what the other group's recollection of past prestige may not have operated equally destructively in the situation. We are divided from each other in our country not only by conflicting interests, but by our memories of past sin and guilt and hurt and resentment. Negro and white remember; north and south remember; they recall stinking slave ships and flowerly lost plantations, old hatred, tears and old courtesy, war and peace, destruction and reconstruction. If we are to achieve community, a common mind, in our nation we cannot do so by trying to forget this remembered past, but only by recalling it; by understanding it more clearly and objectively than we do in our provincial legends; by accepting it and by accepting one another as we are and were. Critical history is for societies the great psychiatric process by which they reconstruct their past—not according to their wishes but in accordance with a surer understanding of what happened to them and what they did, than their uncriticized, emotion-laden, mythical, and legendary memories allow.

We cannot have an invisible ecumenical Church of the spirit unless we are united by our memories; unless we separated groups, divided into confessional and national Churches, remember not only the common past in which we were united, but also that past in which we opposed one another or separated from each other. And to the development of such a community of common, reconciled memory the historical inquiries and teachings of our theological schools have now for a long time been making their great contribution. Some of our history teaching, to be sure, has been undertaken only to continue the separate and separating memories of particular groups. But more of it has demythologized our memories. We see in the light of history the remembered conflicts of Lutherans and Reformed in such a way that the stings of ancient resentments are assuaged. We understand better why our opponents acted as they did, and why we, or our fathers, responded as we did. The struggles of Old Schools and New Schools, Old Lights and New Lights, of churches and sects, of Anglicans and Dissenters, of Evangelicals and Roman Catholics, of Eastern and Western Christians—all our struggles, our past encounters with each other—these take a new form in our mind as we enter into that "dark backward and deep abysm of time" which, left unexplored, functions as our social unconscious—full of unclarified emotions and obscure complexes of love and hate, suppressed anger and grief.

If we have an ecumenical community today in which we are aware of sharing with each a great common past and in which we forgive and are forgiven for the past in which we separated or were separated, rejected or were rejected—then this has come to pass by no supernatural and unmediated grace but by the grace that uses human means and in this case has used the means of the historians' ministrations in our theological schools. Neither they nor we can claim that it was their intention to increase the invisible, intellectual, mental, spiritual, ecumenical Church by giving it a common and reconciled past. But whatever their intentions this effect has come and is increasing.

It is only after such history has done its work that a Roman Catholic can say: "The Reformation was an event not only in the life of Protestantism but of Catholicism also. It was not only the Evangelical Churches that were reformed but the Catholic Church also." Only after history has done its work can the song and the art, the prayers, canticles and orisons, the imagery in stone and color in which the Great Middle Ages of faith expressed their love and gratitude and hope become part of our remembered past, fit to express our devotion and love in the present. The increasingly ecumenical character of our hymnals and prayerbooks, even of our forms of worship, bears witness to the presence of the invisible community, united in memories as well as in its aspirations.

It would be wearisome were I to continue to trace the effect on ecumenical community of the work of theological schools in recent generations through all their special departments. Nor is it likely that I could make out quite so good a case for the other forms of scholarship and teachings as agencies by which the invisible ecumenical community has been fostered. Still, our schools have for a long time nurtured and sustained that community in their study and teaching of dogmatic theology, of Christian and social ethics, of practical theology, of Christian education. Their loyalty to the particular confessional and denominational groups has been high; but they have been loyal in scholarship and teaching to a more universal, more ecumenical truth than the immediate point of view afforded. Their scholars have sought truth, as all good scholars do, with universal intent—to use the phrase a scientist has recently fashioned. And whenever we seek in the Church to know and communicate the truth about ourselves and our faith and our God with such an intent, then we willingly or unwillingly work at the construction of the universal invisible Church.

III

The gratitude we feel in the schools, because some of the materials we have fashioned have been found useful in the building of the world cathedral, is far outweighed—as gratitude is always likely to be—by the sense of new demands upon us. The hope that we may all be one in our acceptance of one another as different members of one body under Christ's headship has increased. Yet it remains a hope; we do not yet see what we hope for. The eschaton to which we look forward has given signs of its incursion into our present. But still with patience and impatience we wait and long for it. And what we wait and long for as members of the Church in this ecumenical age is something more than the reconciliation of the members of Christ's community to each other. These ecumenical institutions, this common mind of ours which we see or feel to be coming to birth—these are but instruments. They do not justify themselves but are justified only by that grace of God which uses them for a purpose beyond all our own conscious and unconscious intentions. Ecumenical Church or national Church, universal Church, confessional Church, visible Church or invisible Church, institutional Church or Church of the common mind—what difference does the form make if the form itself is the end, if the form is not given and sought for the sake of the function?

In this ecumenical age we know well that the realization of an ecumenical Church ideal is not an end with which we can rest content, or even envision as the immediate end-in-view toward which to bend our energies. We may at times in our Church consciousness sing of that Church as the one for which our tears shall fall, our prayers ascend, our toils and cares be given. Then we remember the one who wept over a Jerusalem that harbored along with a few of his disciples many Jews and Romans. We remember that his prayers ascended for those who were of other folds and for his enemies; that he toiled his way up Calvary because God loved the *world*; that he cared for the lost. He reconciled us not to himself or to one another first but to the maker of heaven and earth, to the sovereign power by which and in which all things are and not we only. He sent and sends his Church into all that world, charging it with the ministry of reconciliation: to say to that world in whatever way it can: Be reconciled to God.

This age is less the age of the ecumenical Church than of the ecumenical world. We live in the *oikumene*—the inhabited world, the one economy of mankind—as nations, as citizens, as workers, as thinkers about nature, quite as much as we do as men of the Church. And those who are not members of the Church also live in that one planetary household. Pockets of provincialism doubtless remain. There are those whose real world—the world in which they think and act, in which they find their laws and their goods—is bounded by state, national, cultural or continental boundaries. There are those whose sense of the time in which they live is that of national or religious or cultural history. But the tone and meaning is given to our human world by a leadership in ecumenical churches, ecumenical universities, ecumenical journals, ecumenical institutes of art, ecumenical economic enterprises too, that live subjectively as well as objectively in planetary space, in the community of all mankind, in the time span of human history. This expansion of our existential world into the *oikumene*, the whole inhabited human world, has not come about as a result of our intentions. The human pride which boasts of the expansion of our world as though man had intended this achievement is the pride of ignorance, the arrogance of cocky Chanticleer who thinks the sun obedient to his crowing. No inventor of steam or internal combustion engine, of railroad or airplane; no discoverer of air waves or of neutrons, invented or discovered this world. No statesman planned it. In fear and trembling before what is and what is likely to be we can only say: "What hath God wrought."

But here it is—the *oikumene*—the inhabited world—as the sphere of our living, thinking and acting. Among all the features of this *oikumene* of ours the one that strikes the Christian, churchly eye, most forcibly and painfully is the conflict present in its unity, the irreconciledness that is so evident when the isolated are pressed together in one household. Uneasy, perilous truces of wary, suspicious neighbors characterize political life in the *oikumene*, where communism and Christendom, Islam and the Indian East, Africa and Europe, dwell together within radio-hailing distance of each other, within a missile's throw; where the quarrels in the neighbors' apartments sound clearly through the thin walls. And we know they are not reconciled—these neighbors. They cannot forgive: they cannot accept forgiveness. They cannot forget their ancient rejections and aggressions. All their hands are full of blood and they desire no water for their cleansing.

The ecumenical world of those who are unreconciled to each other is the world of those unreconciled to God. This strange human race has never been reconciled to God—but now its irreconciledness is more conspicuous than ever. On the one hand it manifests itself in the despair that does not know it is despair—the despair of those who try to forget by seeking the enjoyments of the immediate moment or of the near moment to come, the despair that seeks the fulfillment of life's promise in the satisfaction of the lust for a momentary prestige, for a momentary possession, or for an additional few years of personal or national life. On the other hand there is the despair that the most sensitive minds of our ecumenical world voice and communicate— the explicit despair that recognizes no meaning, purpose or hope in this human existence. Individuals and nations live in an ecumenical world—a great household—but the larger it grows the deeper is the suspicion and distrust of the source whence mankind came and of the end toward which it moves. Whether that in which we live and move and have our being, is nothingness, or a great game of chance,—it is the enemy, against which man maintains himself for awhile, unreconciled; in that natural mind which is enmity to God or fear of him as enemy.

These features of the ecumenical age become clearer and more tragic as we move into it more fully. Mankind has become one—and is most divided in its new oneness. It is aware of itself—and of the resentments and guilt that keep it in inner and outer turmoil. And having found itself, it is aware of being lost in its cosmos.

The duty of the Church in this ecumenical age of the world cannot, I am sure, be fulfilled if it is not more fully reconciled within itself and all its parts, to the one God, the God and Father of its Lord Jesus Christ. And it may be that if we become more truly reconciled to him, and to one another in him, we shall then know how to carry on our ministry of reconciliation to those who are near and to those who are far. But even this knowledge will not come automatically, not without painful mental and spiritual struggle.

IV

In the wrestling of the Church today with the question: "How shall we exercise the ministry of reconciliation to the unreconciled *oikumene*?," the seminary may be a focal point. After all the ecumenical councils seeking the reform of the Church at Constance and at Basle, it was in a theological school at Wittenberg that the movement began which reformed not only the Church but gave a new reality to its preaching of reconciliation to the new nations of that day. Oxford and Cambridge, Halle and Utrecht—and many another theological school have been seed-beds, seminaries, not only of sprouting young theologians, but of movements in the Church that spread reconciliation, *metanoia* and faith into the world of their time.

It need, of course, not be so. The commission to go into the world with the ministry of reconciliation may come to men on a hill-top in the hinterlands rather than in a chamber in the capital city. Yet knowing that a sovereign rules over all our intentions, the good as well as the evil, the little as well as the great, we dare not carry on our work in the seminaries in this ecumenical age, without the painful and awful awareness that this Church we serve has been called to serve in the ministry of reconciliation to all the world. We cannot meet the call to this ministry by introducing special courses, by adding to an overloaded curriculum further special inquiries. The question is one about the spirit and the context in which we do all that we do. As the spirit and the context in which Biblical, historical, systematic, and practical theology were studied and taught in the past nurtured the ecumenical mind of Protestant Christendom in recent generations, so the spirit and context in which these studies will be carried on in this ecumenical age of the world, may, we are entitled to believe, prepare the way for that new Reformation which will send us all into the world with a new, spirit-filled way of saying to it: Be reconciled to God.

13

Reformation: Continuing Imperative
[1960]

In a rash or vain moment I accepted *The Christian Century*'s invitation to describe the course of my theological pilgrimage in the recent past. Now that I have made various notes on my recollections of the past and my interests at present I have become more aware than I was of the dubious nature of this enterprise in self-analysis. I am tempted to defensiveness and self-justification by writing an *Apologia pro Vita Sua*; to take myself too seriously as though my theological ideas were representative of more than my own mind; to present myself as more logically consistent than is likely; to present feelings as ideas. To write a wholly honest account would require a more personal confession than is fitting in public discourse. For I suppose that no matter how much all of us work out our thoughts about God and man, life and death, sorrow and joy, in response to common and public events, it is in every case the highly personal, not to say private, experiences that most immediately affect the basic form and formulations of our faith. About such things I neither ought nor want to write. Yet I must redeem my promise and give an account of what I think and how I have come so to think. While, then, I shall attempt to write nothing but the truth, it is clear to me that I shall not tell the whole truth; partly because I do not know it; partly because I owe the whole truth about myself, so far as I know it, only to God. With such warnings to myself and to the reader in mind I begin.

I

The history of my convictions and concern over the last thirty years—not to go back farther—seems to me to be not only continuous but also consistent. Yet I suppose that a purely objective critic of my activities in theological teaching would find reason to believe that I had changed my mind in fairly radical fashion not once but twice during that period. He might say—and I would agree—that in the early 1930s I had given up my connection with that ethics- and religion-centered way of thinking about God and man which is roughly called liberal and that I had affiliated myself with the movement variously called dialectical theology, theology of crisis, neo-orthodoxy and Barthianism. He would, I think, also say—and again I would agree—that in the 1950s I had turned against that movement in its later forms and the tendencies associated with it and had given indications of resuming contact with the earlier modes of theological thought. In support of the latter judgment this objective critic could call attention to the fact that whereas in the 1930s I had written and spo- ken in support of the separation of the church from the world, in the later period I deplored the kind of separation that had taken place; that whereas I had been called a Barthian (though I never accepted the label) I now dissoci- ated myself from Karl Barth's theology; that while once my interest had been strongly oriented toward the church-union movement, I now displayed little concern for the enterprise and looked elsewhere for the reformation of the church. So far as external, rough facts go I would agree with such a critic, but I would disagree with his implied interpretation for I would want to rejoin that nothing in history is fixed—neither liberalism nor orthodoxy, neither church- union nor churchly relevance to the world—and further, that these things have never been causes for me to the extent that loyalty to them was for me a mea- sure of intellectual or personal integrity.

So far as I see it my history has been about as follows: The thirties were for me as for many of my generation in the church the decisive period in the for- mation of basic personal convictions and in the establishment of theological formulations of those convictions. The fundamental certainty given to me then (sad to say, not in such a way that my unconscious as well as my conscious mind has been wholly permeated by it) was that of God's sovereignty. My fun- damental break with the so-called liberal or empirical theology was not due to the fact that it emphasized human sovereignty; to interpret it in that way is to falsify it in unjustifiable fashion. It was rather due to the fact that it defined God primarily in value-terms, as the good, believing that good could be defined apart from God. And now I came to understand that unless being itself, the constitution of things, the One beyond all the many, the ground of my being and of all being, the ground of its "that-ness" and its "so-ness," was trust- worthy—could be counted on by what had proceeded from it—I had no God at all. The change was not a change of definitions of God but of personal rela- tions to my world and the ground of the world as the givenness of life, history, myself. Since I came to that conviction or since it came to me, I have worked considerably at the problem of the nature and meaning of "value" and at efforts to understand the basic relation of the self to that on which it is absolutely dependent. But the old theological phrase, "the sovereignty of God," indicates what is for me fundamental.

Two other convictions were associated for me in those years, as they are now, with divine sovereignty: the one was the recognition of our human lostness, sinfulness, and idolatrousness; the other was the understanding that trust in the ground of being is a miraculous gift. How it is possible to rely on God as inconquerably loving and redeeming, to have confidence in him as purposive person working towards the glorification of his creation and of himself in his works, to say to that great "It": "Our Father who art in heaven"—this remains the miraculous gift. It is the human impossibility which has been made possible, as has also the enlistment of these unlikely beings, these human animals, ourselves, in his cause, the cause of universal creation and universal redemption. So far as I could see and can now see that miracle has been wrought among us by and through Jesus Christ. I do not have the evidence which allows me to say that the miracle of faith in God is worked only by Jesus Christ and that it is never given to men outside the sphere of his working, though I may say that where I note its presence I posit the presence also of something like Jesus Christ.

II

When I write about the nature of faith I am made aware that I brought over into my reorientation of the thirties a kind of methodological conviction that had been formed in me long before, whether in the school of the liberals or simply in modern existence as such: a conviction of the radically historical character of human existence. I am certain that I can only see, understand, think, believe, as a self that is in time. I can understand that, because I live after Christ, I can realize the possibility of a pre-existent, eternal Christ or a second person of the Trinity. But all of this remains theoretical theology for me and I do not see that faith comes to me or to my fellowmen through any doctrines about what lies back of the historical event. It comes to me in history, not in doctrines about it in history.

Some of my critics—and, alas, I myself—have called this position one of historical relativism, which for some people at once means subjectivist. However that may be, if taking our own historicity very seriously means being a liberal then I remained a liberal even in the thirties though religiously speaking I was, and hope I remain, closer to Calvin and Jonathan Edwards than to the theologians who thought they were taking history seriously by speaking about progressive revelation or the development of religion and thus taking themselves out of history as though they could regard it from a vantage point above it—an error which in other forms is present among the orthodox and neo-orthodox as well.

So much for the coming of fundamental religious convictions and theological orientations that make me think of the years between 1930 and 1935 as the time in which I began to think the way I do now. Of course I brought along with me into that period what I had previously learned through experience and study. I did not abandon religious empiricism any more than I abandoned historicism or neo-Kantian epistemology. As we all do I had to rework my past and not leave it behind. But there was another than the personal past to be reworked and reappropriated. As for other men of my theological generation reaction against liberalism meant reactions against its rejection of the social past; its suspicion of tradition; its super-Protestantism in not only passing over the whole medieval period but also the period of the Reformation itself. With the aid of my colleagues and students I turned back to the "Great Tradition." Edwards, Pascal, Luther, Calvin, Thomas, and Augustine became important. But that is the familiar story of the whole generation.

So far as practical churchmanship was concerned it seemed clear to me that whereas the reform of culture (the great concern of the social gospel) remained one of the church's never-ending responsibilities—to which certain theologians were especially called (and I tended to regard my brother, to whom I was indebted for many things, as belonging to that group)—the time called particularly for the reformation of the church, and I was among those for whom this was the special task. As a convinced Protestant (not an anti-Catholic) who saw the sovereignty of God usurped by the spirit of capitalism and nationalism I felt strongly that the times called for the rejection of "Culture Protestantism" and for the return of the church to the confession of its own peculiar faith and ethos.

In that movement of church reformation—dramatized in the struggle of the German Confessing Church with National Socialism—Karl Barth was the decisive spokesman for the primacy of faith, for the independence of the church, for God's transcendence. Barth functioned as the prophet of the movement though he disclaimed the role. The struggle of the Confessing Church in Germany formed the dramatic center of the movement toward church reformation and it is apparent that the consequences of that struggle remain effective in much modern theology, especially on the continent.

III

Now twenty-five years have come and gone since that formative period of the thirties. Much has happened during that time in public and in private spheres—wars and peace, prosperity and adversity, sickness and health, death and life.

Student generations have come and gone with their various climates of theological opinions and their changing needs. But what has happened to me and the events in which I have participated have not changed my fundamental convictions about the sovereignty of God, the lostness of men (though lost in a physically enlarging cosmos) and the gift of forgiveness through faith. Both experience and study have led to some changes in the theological formulation of those convictions. The complex, dynamic, interhuman as well as human-divine interaction of trust and loyalty has excited my wonder and challenged my efforts to understand faith more than ever. Perhaps it is this concentration on faith as trust and loyalty which has led me farther away from the road that many other postliberals—particularly Karl Barth—have taken. So many of them seem to me to have gone back to orthodoxy as right teaching, right doctrine, and to faith as *fides*, as assent; they tend, it seems to me, toward the definition of Christian life in terms of right believing, of Christianity as the true religion, and otherwise toward the assertion of the primacy of ideas over personal relations. When I think about this I have to say to myself that important as theological formulations are for me they are not the basis of faith but only one form of its expression and not the primary one. I discover further a greater kinship with all theologians of Christian experience than with the theologians of Christian doctrine. So I find myself, though with many hesitations, closer to Edwards and Schleiermacher, to Coleridge, Bushnell, and Maurice than to Barth and the dogmatic biblical theology current today in wide circles. To state my understanding of our theological situation briefly: I believe that the Barthian correction of the line of march begun in Schleiermacher's day was absolutely essential, but that it has become an overcorrection and that Protestant theology can minister to the church's life more effectively if it resumes the general line of march represented by the evangelical, empirical, and critical movement. Some new studies in modern theology have convinced me that the movement from Schleiermacher to Troeltsch was by no means so humanistic as its critics have asserted. Existentialism also has served to reinforce my concern for the personal, for the religiously experienced, for the I-Thou relations between God and man and between men. Among contemporary theologians it is Bultmann who above all seems to me to represent this empirical and ethical strain in theology. I feel great kinship with him in his intentions.

IV

Reflections on the sovereignty of God and the forms of faith have led me to see that the problem of the church—at least as it appears today—is not the problem of separating itself only from the idolatries and henotheisms of the world but from its own idolatries and henotheisms. (By "henotheism" I mean the worship of one god who is however the god of an ingroup rather than the ground of all being.) I see our human religion now, whether non-Christian or Christian, as one part of our human culture which like other parts is subject to a constant process of reformation and deformation, of *metanoia* (repentance) and fall. And in that process the deification of the principles of religious society is no less dangerous to men, no less misleading to their faith, than the deification of national or economic principles. If my Protestantism led me in the past to protest against the spirit of capitalism and of nationalism, of Communism and technological civilization, it now leads me to protest against the deification of Scriptures and of the church. In many circles today we have substituted for the religion-centered faith of the nineteenth century a church-centered faith, as though the historical and visible church were the representative of God on earth, as though the Bible were the only word that God is speaking. I do not see how we can witness to the divine sovereignty without being in the church nor how we can understand what God is doing and declaring to us in our public and private experience without the dictionary of the Scriptures, but it seems to me that in our new orthodox movements we are moving dangerously near to the untenable positions against which the Reformation and the eighteenth-century revival had to protest.

While I am speaking of my protests I must include my rejection of the tendency in much postliberal theology to equate theology with Christology and to base on a few passages of the New Testament a new unitarianism of the second person of the Trinity. In my confession of faith, as in that of many men I know, the expression of trust in God and the vow of loyalty to him comes before the acknowledgment of Christ's leadership. I realize that it is not so for all Christians but I protest against a dogmatic formulation that reads me and my companions out of the church.

My primary concern today, however, is not to protest. It is still that of the reformation of the church. I still believe that reformation is a permanent movement, that *metanoia* is the continuous demand made on us in historical life. The immediate reformation of the church that I pray for, look for, and want to work for in the time that may remain to me is its reformation not now by separation from the world but by a new entrance into it without conformity to it. I believe our separation has gone far enough and that now we must find new ways of doing what we were created to do. One side of the situation is that represented by the "world" today, at least the Western world. It seems to me that in that world men have become deeply disillusioned about themselves and are becoming disillusioned about their idols—the nations, the spirit of technological civilization, and so on. They no longer expect the powers in them or around them to save them from destruction (whether through holocaust or boredom) or from the trivialization of an existence that might as well not have been. The so-called underdeveloped nations—including Russia—do not yet know that there is no hope and no glory and no joy in the multiplication of our powers over nature, and we have no way of saving them from going through the experience through which we have passed or are passing. But in the West the most sensitive, if not yet most, men are living in a great religious void; their half-gods have gone and the gods have not arrived. The religious revival we are said to have had in recent years has been, so far as I can see, less a revival of faith in God and of the hope of glory than a revival of desire for faith and of a hope for hope. And it further seems to me that our churches have been filled (our seminaries too) with men and women who are experiencing that emptiness; further, that there is in the society at large a host of similarly minded persons who have not even considered the church as possibly ministering to their need. I am haunted in the presence of that situation by the phrase: "the hungry sheep look up and are not fed."[1]

I do not believe that we can meet in our day the need which the church was founded to meet by becoming more orthodox or more liberal, more biblical or more liturgical. I look for a resymbolization of the message and the life of faith in the One God. Our old phrases are worn out; they have become clichés by means of which we can neither grasp nor communicate the reality of our existence before God. Retranslation is not enough; more precisely, retranslation of traditional terms is not enough; "Word of God," "redemption," "incarnation," "justification," "grace," "eternal life"—is not possible unless one has direct relations in the immediacy of personal life to the actualities to which people in another time referred with the aid of such symbols. I do not know how this resymbolization in pregnant words and in symbolic deeds (like the new words of the Reformation and the Puritan movement and the Great Awakening, like the symbolic deeds of the Franciscans and the social gospelers) will come about. I do count on the Holy Spirit and believe that the words and the deeds will come to us. I also believe, with both the prophets and, of all men, Karl Marx, that the reformation of religion is the fundamental reformation of society. And I believe that nothing very important for mankind will happen as a result of our "conquest" of space or as a result of the cessation of the cold war unless the human spirit is revived within itself.

1. John Milton, *Lycidas* (1638). [Ed.]

Index